MARSH,

America's First Conservationist and Environmentalist.

An Illustrated Biography

by Jane & Will Curtis and Frank Lieberman

Published for THE WOODSTOCK FOUNDATION

by The Countryman Press, Woodstock, Vermont

THE COUNTRYMAN PRESS · WOODSTOCK · VT.

Library of Congress Cataloging in Publication Data

Curtis, Jane,
The world of George Perkins Marsh.

"Printed in association with the Woodstock Foundation"—T.p. verso.
1. Marsh, George Perkins, 1801-1882. 2. Statesmen—United States—Biography. 3. Conservationists—United States—Biography. I. Curtis, Will, II. Lieberman, Frank. III. Title.
E415.9.M185C87 973'.09'94 [B] 82-7394
ISBN 0-914378-89-9 AACR2
ISBN 0-914378-90-2 (pbk.)

Printed in the United States of America

". . . all that I can hope is to excite an interest

in a topic of much . . . importance,

by pointing out the directions

and illustrating the modes

in which human action has been or may be

most injurious or most beneficial

in its influence upon the physical conditions

of the earth we inhabit."

Geo P Marsh

The World of
GEORGE PERKINS

Acknowledgements

We are grateful indeed to the following people who generously assisted us in our search for the photographs, portraits and manuscripts needed in the preparation of this book: —

Diane H. Blumenthal, *National Public Gallery, Washington, D.C.*
Doreen B. Burke, *Metropolitan Museum of Art, New York.*
Connell Gallagher, *Bailey-Howe Library, University of Vermont, Burlington.*
Professor David Lowenthal, *University College London.*
Lt Col E. D. Jeffries Mathews, *British Army, Ret., London.*
Reidun Nuquist, *Vermont Historical Society, Montpelier, Vt.*
Helen Zinkham, *New York Historical Society, New York*
and, finally, thanks to Mary *and* Laurance Rockefeller, *whose Woodstock residence incorporates the childhood home of George Perkins Marsh, and who encouraged us to produce this book on a person and subject close to their hearts.*

The photographs and prints used to illustrate this book have been collected from a wide variety of sources. To all Curators and Staff, our sincere thanks. Credit for each picture is given in the captions in the form of small capital letter abbreviations: —

AA	Archivi Alinari, Florence, Italy
AC	Authors' Collection
AMMH	American Museum of Natural History, New York
BA	Bettmann Archives, New York
DCL	Dartmouth College Library, Hanover, N.H.
GEH	International Museum of Photography, George Eastman House, Rochester, N.Y.
HSM	Harvard Semitic Museum, Cambridge, Mass.
LLA	Lenox (Mass.) Library Association
LOC	Library of Congress, Washington, D.C.
MMA	Metropolitan MBUSEUM OF Art, New York
NA	National Archives, Washington, D.C.
NPL	Norwich (Vermont) Public Library
NYHS	New York Historical Society, New York
NYPL	New York Public Library, New York.
PL	Phyllis Lambert, on loan to the Canadian Centre for Architecture, Montreal
DL	Professor David Lowenthal, University College London
PMS	Peabody Museum of Salem, Mass.
QL	Quechee (Vermont) Public Library
SI	Smithsonian Institute, Washington, D.C.
WHS	Woodstock (Vermont) Historical Society
UVM	Bailey-Howe Library, University of Vermont, Burlington
VHS	Vermont Historical Society, Montpelier

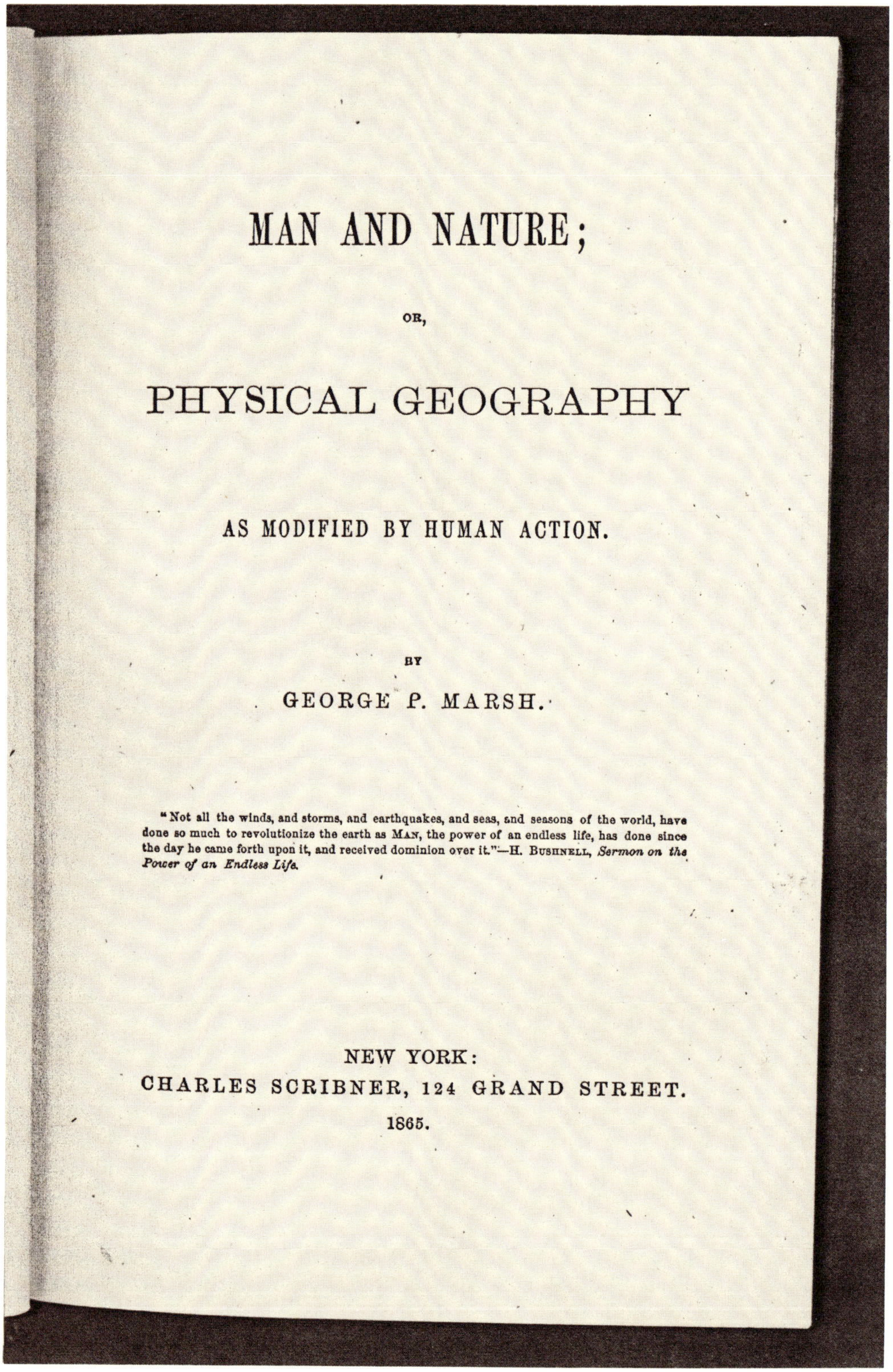

MAN AND NATURE;

OR,

PHYSICAL GEOGRAPHY

AS MODIFIED BY HUMAN ACTION.

BY

GEORGE P. MARSH.

"Not all the winds, and storms, and earthquakes, and seas, and seasons of the world, have done so much to revolutionize the earth as MAN, the power of an endless life, has done since the day he came forth upon it, and received dominion over it."—H. BUSHNELL, *Sermon on the Power of an Endless Life.*

NEW YORK:
CHARLES SCRIBNER, 124 GRAND STREET.
1865.

Title page of MAN AND NATURE *AC*

OVER a hundred years ago we were warned of our wasteful ways by a Vermont lawyer, George Perkins Marsh. In a remarkable book called, *Man and Nature, Physical Geography as Modified by Human Action* published in 1864, Marsh foretold our problems and developed a scientific study to deal with them, ecology, the concept of the interrelationship between organisms and the environment.

When the first Europeans came to North America, the continent was rich in natural resources, rich beyond the wildest dreams. Clear fish-filled streams, primeval forests, grass as far as the eye could see, an earth filled with minerals; all was here for the taking. The frontiersman, the farmer, the business entrepreneur never doubted that such bounties would last forever.

In *Man and Nature,* Marsh anticipated the crisis in pollution, over-population and vanishing resources and stated that man was no asset to the earth. "Even now," said Marsh, "we are breaking up the floor and the wainscotting and doors and window frames of our dwelling to warm our bodies and seethe our pottage." These prophetic words were written in 1864. Today we know that we have recklessly let acres of fertile crop and range land the size of France wash or blow away, or have allowed it to disappear under suburban sprawl. The cost of cleaning up our polluted environment is enormous, but most frightening to our 20th century civilization is the realization that the sources of inexpensive energy on which that civilization is based are drying up at an alarming rate. We have indeed used our capital of natural resources in a most careless and thoughtless manner.

George Perkins Marsh was without doubt one of the most extraordinary of beings, a man of boundless enthusiasms and massive intelligence. In his long life he managed to write a definitive book on the origin of the English language, a Scandinavian grammar, and to form one of the first collections of art in America. He was also a bankrupt businessman, who at the age of 55 regarded himself as a failure. He headed the commission that designed the present Vermont State House in Montpelier, when the old one burned down in 1857. He helped to found the Smithsonian Institution. The final design of the Washington Monument was his. He wrote a book urging the use of camels in the American desert. He was an expert instrument maker, a lawyer, a politician, a master of twenty languages, a Minister to Turkey and finally, the first American Minister to the newly formed Kingdom of Italy, a post he held for twenty-one years, a record unsurpassed by any other American diplomat. But of far greater importance, he was this country's first environmentalist.

Charles Marsh argued cases in the courthouse on the right, in this earliest photograph of Woodstock. WHS *Below: Visiting lawyers "put up" at the Eagle Hotel, an 1830 woodcut.* WHS *Opposite: Marshland Farm, in Quechee, built by George's grandfather, Joseph Marsh.* QL

WHEN the Charles Marsh family celebrated the birth of their new son George in 1801, the village of Woodstock, Vermont had long since shed its frontier beginnings. It was the foremost town in the county, important in manufacturing and banking, and the center of the law profession.

The village was much as it is today. Classic, handsome, white clapboard or mellow brick, the substantial houses still cluster about the tree-shaded green. On Sunday the townsfolk hear the clangor of Paul Revere's bells, for Woodstock boasts of four that were cast in his foundry. Of white-trimmed brick, the courthouse stands foursquare, proclaiming that Woodstock is the Shire Town of Windsor County. The spacious inn is the fourth to be built on the same site since 1792; the old gilded eagle still perches above the entrance as it did over its predecessors. Quintessence of New England, the village nestles between rolling wooded hills while the Ottauquechee flows gracefully through its midst and on past fertile meadows to join the Connecticut River.

The Marshes weren't Woodstock folk. They had come from Connecticut, as did most immigrants, to what was then the frontier, considering themselves several cuts above the hard-scrabble settlers. Their first home, Marshland Farm, still stands several miles to the East on the banks of the Ottauquechee River just before it plunges into the Que-

chee Gorge. As befitting a prosperous man, George Perkins Marsh's grandfather, Joseph, was elected the new state's first Lieutenant Governor, establishing the family's reputation for public service.

Joseph's son, Charles, after graduating from nearby Dartmouth College, studied law with the renowned Tapping Reeves of Litchfield, Connecticut, then set up practice in Woodstock. Prominent young Mr. Marsh was also the first lawyer in town and being able, soon became prosperous. With his wife and little son Charles, he moved into the large comfortable house he had built, perched on the side of Mt. Tom and looking out over the fertile meadows of his farm.

The young lawyer was also a shrewd business entrepreneur. He organized a profitable company to operate a turnpike connecting Woodstock with towns in the interior. The first bridge over the Ottauquechee River was laid out by him and he planned the new courthouse, the first of three to be built in the town. His farm was the finest in the region.

His young wife died early, leaving him with two children. In 1798 Charles married the recently widowed Susan Perkins Arnold, daughter of Elisha Perkins, of Plainfield, Connecticut, widely known as "Terrible Tractor" Perkins. The ingenious doctor, intrigued by that new phenomenon, electricity, had invented a device, "a tractor," with

Opposite: Woodstock's Village Green. WHS
Above: The Marshes brick house on the slopes of Mt. Tom, still bare from the fire of 1800. WHS *Left. A closer view of the Marsh house.* DL *Below: Charles Marsh's bridge over the Ottauquechee River.* WHS

which he stroked rheumatic pains from stiffened joints. His grandson George may have inherited some of the doctor's interest in science.

Susan brought to the large house her own little daughter and in time the rooms were filled with five more children, George Perkins being the second son and child born to the couple in 1801.

Not much is known of Susan Marsh, but her son George always spoke of her sympathetic nature and bountiful housekeeping. It must have taken an energetic woman to cope with her houseful of small children, her servants, her busy husband and to entertain all those who came to Woodstock. For it was with the Marshes, the town's most prominent family, that notable visitors expected to stay.

We can only imagine what the house was like in those early years of the 19th Century. It probably had large square rooms, carefully paneled woodwork, and furnishings in the elegant style of the times. There was a library, well-stocked with leather-bound books, and a big kitchen in whose open fireplace the family's meals were cooked. The rooms were heated by fireplaces as well for stoves had yet to come into use.

The foremost influence on George's mind and character was his father. He was a handsome man, tall, lean and severe looking. With the only trained legal mind in the county, he soon brought order to the badly organized court. In addition, well-educated Charles Marsh was a civilizing influence in the small up-country community. He had scant

Charles Marsh's portrait, by Woodstock painter, Benjamin Franklin Mason, is prominently displayed in the courtroom of Woodstock's courthouse. AC

patience for the bumbling of those less intelligent than himself. A stern Calvinist, he looked with disapproval on evil-doers. To win love and approval in the Marsh household one had to take great care in the discharge of the tasks assigned and also appreciate booklearning for its own sake. Facts were precious things to be stored in the mind and used pointedly at the proper moment. All his life George Perkins Marsh loved abstruse facts and was wont to fill his lectures so full of these treasures that his audiences sometimes fell asleep.

Susan Marsh recalled often seeing her seven-year-old George crouched under a table to read a volume of the encyclopedia because it was too heavy for him to carry to better light. At that age he had begun to study Greek and Latin with his older brother. By the time the family discovered that he had been suffering from headaches and could scarce see across the valley, the damage had been done. All his life he remained extremely nearsighted and subject to recurring eye trouble that left him for weeks unable to stand light. His eyes had to be covered with folds of black silk. The immediate consequences for the child was the banning of books for four years. To George this decree, at first a disaster, was one of the fortunate events in his life, for it set him on the path that would eventually lead him to write *Man and Nature.* The frail boy whose head seemed unnaturally adult for his slender frame was turned forcibly out of doors. Banished from the library he joined the swarm of brothers, cousins, and village boys that roamed the countryside. The Marsh's fields, the rocky Ottauquechee River, and the hill behind his father's house were their playing fields. Instead of reading about the world around him, George was compelled to observe and to explore it for himself and to fit the observed facts into a larger whole. He acquired a passionate love of nature. He soon knew the note of every bird, the track of every animal that lived in the woods. He once described himself as "forest born: — the bubbling brook, the trees, the flowers, the wild animals were to me persons, not things." A great oak, he once said, had a better claim to respectability than many humans he knew. The outdoors became a physical need; in his late 70's he was still walking in the Alps. His wife told of how as a boy he delighted in the feeling of rain on his head; as a stately old gentleman, if caught in a shower, he would often take off his tall silk hat and let the downpour drench him, a source of amusement, she said, to his friends.

In the forty-odd years since the first settler had come to live in Woodstock, the landscape had changed. Pioneer wastefulness and the need for fuel had stripped the trees from the hills. It took upwards of forty cords of wood each year for a large household to heat and cook with their inefficient fireplaces. Observant of the natural world, George

Opposite: Shorn hills rise above the fertile Ottauquechee Valley. Below: The Pogue, a hidden lake on the summit of Mt. Tom, where George played with his friend, Hiram Powers, whose home, on barren College Hill, is shown at right. All WHS

clearly saw the result of this deforestation. He noticed that the spring freshets grew increasingly violent as more trees were cut from the hills. The floods finally carried away his father's sawmill. He and his friends saw too, that deforestation had another effect. The spring floods gave way to droughty summer trickles and the fishing became worse and worse as the years went on. The bared hills could no longer let the stored moisture make its way down slowly and evenly.

His father, also an observant man, had a part in George's out-of-doors education. He would take the boy with him when having to attend court in another town. George remembered one such trip. "I was four-and-a-half years old at the time and sat on a little stool between my father's knees in the two-wheeled chaise in which he always drove. That 'one-horse shay' must have been as strong as the old deacon's, for the roads in those days were shocking. But I little heeded that, for to my mind the whole earth lay spread out before me. My father pointed out the most striking trees as we passed them, and told me how to distinguish their varieties. I do not think I ever afterward failed to know one forest tree from another. He called my attention to the general configuration of the landscape, pointed out the direction of the different ranges of the hills, told me how the water gathered on them and ran

ACE OFFICE

Opposite page: Trees were cut heedlessly to supply wood for hungry fireplaces. NHHS
Ox teams drew huge loads of firewood to be sold "down-street" in Woodstock. WHS
Log jams, such as the one shown above on the White River, near Sharon, were a common sight, VHS, *but such feckless cutting often resulted in Spring floods.* VHS

down their sides, and where the mountain streams would likely be found. But what struck me, perhaps most of all, he stopped his horse on top of a steep hill, bade me notice how the water there flowed in different directions, and told me such a point was called a watershed . . . . . I never forgot that word, or any part of my father's talk that day."

When George and his friends clambered up the steep slope of his father's Mt. Tom, its rocky summit was barren. The mountain had been burned over the year before George was born and vegetation had still not been re-established. As the boys played, George observed how the tiny saplings, struggling to grow, died from lack of nourishment. The topsoil, with no roots to restrain it, had been gradually washed away from the scorched mountainside by every rain.

In these ways the basic education of the geographer/naturalist was laid down. Perhaps without noticing it, George was establishing in the recesses of his mind a consciousness of the interconnection between water courses, saplings and bared hills. He possessed an unusual ability to take in the character and meaning of natural events, at an age when most boys are concerned solely with games and play.

Formal education hardly counted in Marsh's life. His immense erudition was due to his own life-long search for knowledge. Because of frequent epidemics, the local grammar school was closed as often as it was open. George spent a few unhappy and boring months at Phillips Academy, Andover, Massachusetts, performing the dreary task of abstracting the headmaster's dull sermons. But readings with his father and brother prepared him so well for Dartmouth that he entered at the age of 15.

The small college, five day's journey by wagon from the nearest city, boasted in its bulletin that ". . . its remoteness from large cities and towns and consequent freedom from many temptations . . . and allurements of dissapations and vice make it one of the safest. . . ."Distance also made it one of the dullest. Buried deep in the hill country, it had been sheltered from the liberating winds of change blowing through more urban institutions.

Five professors taught the antiquated curriculum unchanged since the days of Founder Eleazar Wheelock. Greek and Latin, mathematics and theology, moral philosophy and metaphysics — such was the fare proferred the 150 students.

Already proficient in classics and mathematics, George mastered French, Italian, Spanish and Portuguese on his own. By the time he graduated, he could speak those languages fluently. On the side, he gave Professor Ebenezer Adams badly needed hints on astronomy, the only course in science.

Above: Dartmouth College in the 1820s, a lithograph by Nathaniel Currier, DCL, *and right: Portrait of George Marsh shortly after his graduation from Dartmouth, by G. P. A. Healy.* DLC

Norwich Military Academy, from Zadock Thompson's 1824 Gazeteer of Vermont. NPL

Marsh's years at Dartmouth set the pattern he was to follow throughout his long life, a life devoted to the independent study of the many subjects which aroused his interest. A classmate remembered, "He was a great and good scholar, and everybody loved and admired him, but he was so intensely delighted with his books that he made few intimate friendships."

Graduation in 1820 found him still undecided about his future. Consequently he accepted an offer to teach English at Norwich Military Academy across the river in Vermont. A great inducement was that the Dartmouth Library was nearby. But military students were poor fuel for Marsh's burning torch of educational zeal. Like his father, he had scant patience with dullness and found the quiet of the library a welcome refuge from a schoolroom filled with bored young men. As before, he overdid it and his near-sighted eyes again gave out. Sessions in New York and Philadelphia with the medical experts of the time left him rather worse off, so back he came to Woodstock and his family. For three years he studied law under his father's or brother's tuition, and attended court when an important case was being argued. Most of the days he was outdoors again. This period, he later said, was one of the seasons of greatest growth of his life. It was a time when his remarkable powers of observation were still further developed.

After examination by a committee of three, including Senator Jacob Collamer, he was admitted to the bar as an attorney of the Windsor County Court, and at once set out for Burlington, where he lived for the next thirty-five years. Had Marsh found Woodstock a bit confining, living under the eye of his tyrannical father and of his older brother, both successful lawyers? At any rate, on October 28, 1825, the Burlington *Northern Sentinel* ran this notice: "B. F. Bailey and G. P. Marsh, attorneys-at-law, have formed a co-partnership under the firm of Bailey and Marsh, and will attend to the business of their profession at the office hitherto occupied by B. F. Bailey in Pearl St."

Burlington, the "Queen City" of Vermont, on the other side of the state from Woodstock, was rapidly growing; it already numbered 1650 souls when Marsh set up practice there. Its site was dramatic, showing a broad sweep from the top of a ridge where the university was located, down to Lake Champlain, with its superb vistas across the water to the Adirondacks. Schooners and canal boats crowded the docks and moorings, ready to load lumber for the journey through the Whitehall-Albany canal that joined the lake with the Hudson. Houses and buildings were as handsome as the location; the first log huts had long since been replaced by imposing mansions for the leading families. Charles Dickens, visiting in 1842, and not always enthusiastic about America, said of the city that it was "an exquisite achievement of neatness, elegance, and order." Henry James called Burlington "the most truly

Burlington, Vermont, an early view from College Hill, looking across Lake Champlain. UVM

Above: A very early photograph of Burlington's City Hall Park. UVM
Below: The shipping trade on Lake Champlain, using freight boats such as these, made Burlington the largest, most prosperous town in Vermont. UVM
Opposite: Looking south on Church Street. UVM

charming of New England country towns." Then too, there was for Marsh the added attraction of the University of Vermont which, under the presidency of his cousin, James Marsh, had gained national reputation as one of the most advanced and liberal schools in the country.

The partnership with Bailey was successful from the beginning. The studious Marsh did most of the exacting, sedentary work, while Bailey, attractive, brilliant, popular, brought in the business, chiefly civil suits.

In 1832 Bailey unexpectedly died of the measles, and Marsh's legal career did not long survive him. George was bored by fools; he was contemptuous of sharp dealers; and often having one or the other species to deal with as clients, he did not hesitate to let them know how he felt about them. A new partnership with his brother-in-law, Wyllys Lyman, from Hartford, Vermont, was not a great success. Marsh did not really seem to have his heart in the law; he said of himself that he "lacked the special gifts of the profession and (was) but an indifferent practitioner." He finally closed his office in 1842.

Yet the Burlington years were times of fulfillment and friendships, as well as of tragedy and failure. They were years when Marsh veered between a life in the law, politics, business, and scholarship. The tragedy, when it came, was all but overwhelming.

In 1828, he had married the lively Harriet Buell, daughter of a prominent landowner, and with his flourishing law partnership and his congenial tasks in a little house on Pearl Street, he was happier than he was ever to be again. The couple was thrilled that a child was on the way when Marsh's friend, Dr. Benjamin Lincoln, warned him that Harriet had a heart defect that might prove serious. Marsh kept the news secret, for Harriet seemed well and happy. Charles was born, and the proud young father declared him "of good promise intellectually." After the difficult birth of another son, George Ozias, her condition worsened so much that Harriet asked to be taken to specialists. Marsh, fearing that the journey would be dangerous, tried to dissuade her. In New York they were told that her ailment was indeed serious, but another worry caused them to rush back to Burlington. Charles was desperately ill with scarlet fever. The delicate mother was relieved to find the child apparently better, but the strain had been too much for her weak heart. She died after only five years of marriage.

The stricken young husband now had to nurse Charles, who had had a relapse and became deaf as a result of his high fever. The father would write on a slate to answer the child's questions. Years afterwards, when the house on Pearl Street was being sold, the old slate was found

in the attic with Marsh's words to Charles still legible. The boy died eleven days after his mother's death.

Marsh took baby George to Woodstock to be cared for by the grandmother. Then he shut himself in his empty house in Burlington to mourn. For almost two years he isolated himself, avoiding all but necessary business contacts, eating his meals in a hotel, spending every evening in his lonely house. He said, "It was well for me that business drove me into a constant succession of severe labors of a very engrossing character. This only saved me from madness, for I was never alone for more than a year without bursting into a fit of sorrow, for even my dreams were full of death."

During the long sleepless nights, he found a measure of distraction in studying the Scandinavian languages, a study begun while he was teaching at Norwich Academy. The Danish linguist, Carl Rafn, when appealed to for help in obtaining books, soon had 50 to 100 volumes arriving every month at Marsh's door, "but proh dolor! (Anglice: alas for my dollars!) the price of some of them are such as to astound even me, accustomed as I am to being fleeced in this way!" By 1849 he had amassed one of the largest collections of Scandinavian literature in this country. The Icelandic language was his specialty. He published his

Marsh lived in this simple house, center left, on the corner of Pearl and Church Streets for 35 years. He added a library ell to house his growing collection of books and prints. UVM

translation of the *Compendious Grammar of the Old-Northern or Icelandic Language,* and translated articles and poems from Danish and Swedish, as well. His name among men of letters began to be known as that of the foremost Scandinavian scholar in North America.

Marsh's preoccupation with all things Scandinavian inspired a lecture he gave with the strange title "The Goths in New England," a production that received a good deal of criticism. It reflected some prevalent ideas of the early decades of the 19th Century in America: romanticism, patriotism, religious prejudice. The very presence of the word "Goth" reveals one side of Marsh's complex nature. He believed that the ancient Goths, by which he meant the Scandinavians, had, when the Danes ruled Britain, imparted all that was fine and good to England. The Puritans, spiritual descendants of the Danes, fleeing the popish Angelican Church, had brought to New England their love of freedom, moral purity, industriousness. The harsh climates of Scandinavia and New England had fostered these characteristics. This theorizing explains his fear of taking people of alien climates into the Union, when he later argued against the annexation of the Southwest. "So long as the same mountains and plains and stormy shores shall be exposed to the same fierce extremes of cold and heat, so long will the character of New England be conspicuous for the traits which now distinguish it." As for the fast-growing cities swelling with the waves of Catholics fleeing Ireland and Germany, he feared they were filled with the "corruptions of Popery." He had no truck with the Know-Nothing Party of the 1840's, whose members when interrogated always replied that they "knew nothing." He scoffed at their ". . . foolish machinery of badges and wigwams, sachem's oaths, secrets and other like silliness. . . ." But he agreed with ". . . their avowed principles of . . . restriction of the right of naturalization and resistance to Catholic encroachments. . . ."

Only in the rural countryside, moreover, could virtue be found. Americans must be aware of their Puritan heritage and resist "every foreign heresy or folly in religion." One friend chided, "You credit the Puritans with much of your modern thought, which they never had. . . . Why, if you were compelled to live with the real Puritans, George Marsh, you would soon be driven to hang yourself to escape being burned by them!" In later years, as he grew less provincial, he modified his ideas concerning patriotism and religion, but he always retained his Calvinist's distrust of Catholicism.

Little by little, as a turtle emerges from his shell, Marsh once again moved about in the society of men. The lively circle gathered at the University of Vermont was just the stimulus he needed. President

The University of Vermont, situated high above the town, attracted scholars and writers such as Marsh's good friend, gazeteer Zadock Thompson, at left. Cousin James Marsh, President of the University, introduced Transcendental Philosophy to America. All UVM

Caroline Crane, left, at the time of her marriage, and right, a later sketch of Caroline by Minter Kellog. Both UVM

James Marsh, believing that the Green Mountain boys deserved a college education, had liberalized the entrance requirements and done away with the mechanical methods of textbook teaching. He gathered about him a group of distinguished scholars and introduced such subjects as philosophy, notably Transcendentalism, and the natural sciences. Marsh found himself enjoying botanical rambles, evening-long discussions of mathematics and music, and conversations with Zadock Thompson, born in Bridgewater just to the west of Woodstock. Thompson, geologist, historian, and scholar, a man with almost as many interests as Marsh himself, was the author of the *History of Vermont, Natural, Civil and Statistical,* still an indispensable book of reference.

Nor was female society lacking. He met and fell in love with a dark-eyed young woman named Caroline Crane, sister of the Reverend Silas Crane, in whose school for young ladies she taught. Caroline, 15 years George's junior, liked his erect bearing, firm mouth and serious grey eyes. In the prime of life, Marsh had filled out his frame and become an impressive figure. He wooed her with amusing letters when she left for New York to teach school — perhaps to give herself time to

Caroline brought a light touch into Marsh's life. Croquet was a popular pastime of the day. VHS

think about marriage to this man so different from the ordinary young suitor. He painted a rueful, gloomy picture of himself subjected to ". . . that semi-annual operation yclept by country housewives as 'house-cleaning.' A pail of soapsuds with a mop in it, a room with two windows out, and a grim virago in a short gown putting dirt to rout . . . inspire me with terror." A doleful, lonely letter explained ". . . I believe no man was ever so constituted as to require the society of a sympathizing friend more imperiously than I. I do not know how it is, but I not only feel the necessity of communicating my thoughts and feelings, but it seems to me I cannot even see sightworthy objects alone."

They were married in 1839. In Caroline he had found the perfect wife, highly intelligent, and one who shared his tastes. His immense erudition never overwhelmed her. She had her own literary pursuits. Together with her husband or by herself, she translated Swedish and German verse and published a book of her own poems, *Wolfe of the Knoll,* highly regarded by critics in her day.

It was she who influenced Marsh toward the feminist cause, long before it was fashionable to do so. She had been drawn into the circle of the avant-guarde Blackwell family through Anna Blackwell, a teacher at Silas Crane's school. Anna's famous sister, Dr. Elizabeth Blackwell, America's first woman doctor, became a good friend of the Marsh's, visiting them in Florence and Rome, and keeping them apprised of women's struggle for equality. In 1874 Dr. Blackwell wrote from London that she knew Marsh would be interested in the establishment of a clinic for women, in the rapid growth of cooperative housing, and in the visit she had made to Girton College for Women at Cambridge. Marsh had become vitally interested in women's education. "If we would make a people great and free, we must, above all, promote the education of its women." And again: "Make women legally and socially the peer of men, afford her equal if not identical means of education."

Caroline, though an invalid for a good part of her married life, never allowed her invalidism to restrict her husband's activities. She suffered from a variety of ailments that left her unable to walk or, at times, to read for more than a few minutes, but she always accompanied him on his travels, borne on a litter in Syria, boosted onto a shuffling camel in Egypt, trundled in a wheelbarrow over Alpine snowdrifts.

One of her greatest assets was her clearheadedness in the face of trouble. Marsh, who certainly had his share of disappointment and tragedy, was liable to indulge in bouts of self-pity, to feel himself overwhelmed by his woes, real and imagined. After two financial entanglements, occurring close together, he became almost paranoid. Caroline, with her calm good sense, buoyed him up, assuring him that his troubles weren't that bad and not to give in to self-pity.

Best of all, under her light touch the withdrawn, solitary widower became a more genial being, more tolerant of others' shortcomings. The once sad little house became again a happy, lively place, regulated by the literary pursuits of its inhabitants. The new young bride found that the furnishings provided by her studious husband were of the plainest and that every inch of the walls was covered by books, or by his growing collection of etchings. Fortunately she liked books and art.

A daily schedule evolved, which was held to as far as possible throughout Marsh's life. Winter or summer he was up by five and lit a fire in his library. Then, turning to his table, on which were piled five or six volumes in different languages, he would devote an hour or so first to one, and then to another. After an eight o'clock breakfast, he set off for his office, returning at one for his midday meal. The "country dinner" that Caroline provided necessitated a nap, and a little after two he would return to his law practice for a few hours. The evenings were cozy and quiet, reading aloud to Caroline or playing with young George, who had been brought back to Burlington.

In spite of these formidable arrangements for productivity, Marsh complained that owing ". . . to weakness of sight, business cares and domestic sorrows, I have absolutely no time for regular study or thought since I left college . . . I have lost much of the precision and accuracy, and much of the extent of the general knowledge, of my youth; my powers of observation have been weakened by disease, my enthusiasm cooled and my spirit sobered by labors, disappointments and griefs." One wonders what he expected of himself.

With the death of Harriet and her father, Marsh had inherited a good deal of valuable property and in addition, the firm of Lyman and Marsh bought extensive tracts of wood and pastureland, not only in Burlington, but in surrounding towns. Favorable tariffs on wool had raised the demand for sheep and Marsh soon had thousands on his beautiful farm in Shelburne. In the summer he drove out almost daily, suggesting new methods of agriculture to his tenants and enjoying every detail of farming procedure.

Finding the practice of law more and more boring, and perhaps infected by the booming economy of the region, Marsh looked to the business world to provide an adequate income. In the end all his

Merino sheep, noted for their luxuriant wool, as shown on a breeder's handbill. VHS

Before clipping, sheep were thoroughly washed. NYPL *The wool was then processed in Marsh's mill on the Winooski River, seen in this contemporary sketch.* UVM

money-making schemes came to naught: woolen manufacturing, marble quarrying, railroad investment — all failed disastrously. For most of his life Marsh worried about the lack of money. Even in his later years, when he was assured of an income as a diplomat, he continued to be haunted by the spectre of insolvency.

His first venture started auspiciously. Part of the land that Lyman and Marsh had bought on speculation was that which bordered the Winooski River. Swift and shallow, the river meanders through the meadows that separate Camel's Hump from the Green Mountain Range and, near the town of Winooski, drops 38 feet to the level of Lake Champlain. These falls were in the parcel owned by the partners. Earlier, the brothers Ira and Ethan Allen had seen the river's potential water power and had built two dams there, both eventually washed out by spring floods. The falls had remained unused for 15 years, when they attracted Marsh's attention. Vermont was pre-eminently a wool-growing state; why should it not manufacture its own wool, and why should this not be done on the Winooski Falls? The wealthy businessmen of the city took a favorable view of the project. The Burlington Mill Co. was incorporated and to facilitate access to the falls, a road was built with a good deal of the partners' own money and Marsh's sweat. Marsh himself laid out and superintended the road, "often lifting heavy logs and stones in order to quicken the zeal of his Irish laborers."

The panic of 1837 stopped work for a while and Marsh took a trip west to see for himself the promised land that was attracting so many Vermonters. It was full of promise, he said, but the privations entailed by living there would be fatal to his intellectual growth.

The seven-story mill was intended to take the wool as it came from the animal's back and see it through the 211 stages of manufacture to final packaging as cloth. Twenty steam-heated tenants' houses were built for the laborers and, as the Burlington *Sentinel* boasted, the place would soon rival Lowell, Massachusetts, then the most up-to-date mill town in the country.

Alas for the partners, the mill ran into trouble at once. A bad fire in 1838 did great damage before it had even opened, and the next spring an ice jam injured the machinery. Such could be repaired, but an unforeseen act of Congress proved disastrous. As a result of the tariff cuts of 1839, the price of wool dropped so low that farmers let their sheep die during the winter rather than spend money to feed them. Marsh had to sell his manufactured cloth for less than he had paid for the raw wool the previous spring. A little help came with the tariff of 1842, but that of 1846 was ruinous, once more totally removing protection from domestic woolens. There was nothing for Marsh to do but sell his mill

Caroline's sister, Lucy Crane, poses, while George and Caroline hold hands in this photograph taken shortly after their marriage. LOC

at a punishing loss. Many ruined farmers moved west and land prices tumbled in Vermont.

Marsh undoubtedly lacked the sense of timing which distinguishes the successful businessman; canniness in choosing trust-worthy associates also seemed to be missing in him. Most probably, he did not pay enough attention to business affairs because his other pursuits were always more engrossing.

Of all his misadventures, his heavy investment in the Vermont Central Railroad was the one that haunted him for the rest of his life. The inland waterways that had made Burlington prosperous were being superseded in the '30's by the iron horse. The first locomotive of the Vermont Central Railroad chartered to link Vermont with the seacoast markets and the Canadian forests, steamed into Burlington in 1849. The city's shipping trade was shattered but Marsh, looking to the future, hoped to recoup some of his losses and bought all the railroad stock he could. Soon after this he was sent to Turkey as U. S. Minister, leaving his brother-in-law, Wyllys Lyman to look after his investments — a deplorable decision. Lyman, a weak man, was no match for the unscrupulous railroad magnates who were out to wring all the profits from the company for themselves. The debacle came later, but the mistake was made when he trusted Lyman.

He showed no better judgment when he ventured into tool-and-instrument-making. As a child, holding his brother Lyndon's hand, he had watched the carpenters build his father's house, looked at their tools, observed the growing piles of stone and mortar. All his life George loved to handle brass and steel, wood and glass; he spent hours designing instruments of glass and ivory for measuring and surveying. He hoped to patent them. The patent office told him his ideas were 35 years too late. In an effort to recoup his railroad losses, he then involved himself in still another enterprise, quarrying marble; that too proved a calamity.

One reason for his failures was ambivalence. Marsh liked to think of himself as a successful man of affairs, but at the same time he rather scorned those who gave their lives to grubbing for money. Could they not see how many things there were in the world more fascinating than money? To do anything well requires a person's full attention. By dividing his, Marsh had to spend years fighting his way out of bankruptcy and the prospect of poverty was before his eyes during much of his life.

In what he truly loved to do or think about, Marsh was preeminent. At a time when the frontier ethos still fostered a disdain for the arts, Marsh was making himself an authority, particularly on the history of engraving. "When I was little more than a baby, my mother brought me from Boston an ivory horse with gilded mane, tail and hoofs . . . to me it

was a revelation and from that day I date that love of art which has afforded me so much enjoyment since." His collection of the best works of every engraver of note, particularly those of Dürer, made it the choicest if not the largest in the country. Even when his finances were at their lowest ebb, he could still squeeze some money for a particularly fine work. To Caroline he wrote, "I fear you will think I am becoming *'pazzo per l'arte'* (mad about art), but when you consider from what lower professional cares and business perplexities it partially withdraws me, you will rejoice that I am now making art . . . my principal hobby." During the particularly trying summer of 1845, when everything was going wrong with his business affairs, his greatest success was finding some "remarkably fine engravings which I could not resist." His collection, sold by Marsh to the Smithsonian, when he needed money, vanished in the fire of 1865.

The art by which he had seen piles of brick and mortar transformed into a handsome four-square house for his father made a lasting impression on the boy. All his life he had a love of architecture, a sure eye for good proportion and a sense of style. As an amateur architect, Marsh made important contributions to the final designs of such public buildings as the Washington Monument and the Vermont State House. In

1879, while living in Rome as American Minister, Marsh learned to his horror that the still unfinished Washington Monument was to be topped off with an enormous statue. Senator Morrill from Vermont had an even more atrocious notion — take the stump down and make a triumphal arch of the stones. Marsh had been to Egypt. He wrote to the Washington Monument Committee that he had sketched all the great obelisks of antiquity, and none had been topped off by statues; "the notion of spitting a statue on the sharp point of the pyramidion is supremely absurd." His criticism prevailed, and the monument remains a simple shaft.

There is yet one more career to add to the list of those he adorned. It is difficult, as Caroline said of that period, to tell what his principal occupation was: law, business, or scholarship. He had been a lawyer, a farmer, a wool manufacturer, a quarry man, an architect, an art collector, a diplomat, a would-be inventor, a linguist, and he had also served a term in the Supreme Legislative Council of Vermont in the lonely years after his first wife died.

Marsh was that august body's youngest member, but his ability to impress others with his intellectual prowess soon made him its leader. Although he believed in ameliorating harsh debtor's laws, he was firmly against abolishing the debtor's prisons. To do so would furnish "no satisfactory substitute for the security of the creditor . . . ." His persuasive words killed the reform measure for the time being.

The Washington Monument, opposite, begun in 1848, remained an unfinished stump until 1884, when, largely due to Marsh, it was given its present form and this cap was finally put into place. LOC

He had made his mark in Vermont's General Assembly. Would he now consider running for Congress?

According to Caroline, it was an impressive speech Marsh made before the Mechanics' Institute of Burlington, in which he extolled the benefits of modern inventions, that first caused his friends to consider him as a candidate. Although Marsh hoped that his large landholdings would sometime make him wealthy, the wool factory was then swallowing up all his income to keep it going. He was finding his law practice more and more irksome, and his clients were all too aware of that fact. A long-cherished plan to go to Europe had to be put off in part for financial reasons, in part because of the illness and deaths of tuberculosis of his brother Joseph and his favorite sister, Sarah. His sister Anne and a niece had already died of the dread disease. Vermont winters were hard on Caroline; he, himself, would benefit from the softer climate of Washington and be able to take exercise. The decision was: whether to return full time to the practice of law so as to support his family, or to do something else that would bring in an income until business conditions improved.

By 1834 the Whig party, later the Republican party, was led by "Black Dan" Webster and Henry Clay. A collection of anti-populist, anti-Jackson forces, it was held together by a common interest in property rights and naturally favored protective tariffs. Marsh, as a mill

Left: George Perkins Marsh, freshman Congressman. Opposite: "Black Dan" Webster, Secretary of State and America's most famous orator. Right: Henry Clay opposed the annexation of Texas; an unsuccessful Presidential candidate, he was beaten by Polk on this issue. All LOC

owner in deep trouble because of cheap, imported wool, believed he could exert some influence that would be of benefit, not only to himself, but to the distressed New England states whose industries were failing. Congress, dominated by the southern Democrats who wanted cheap cloth, had lowered the protective tariffs, with disastrous effects on the manufacturing North. Marsh was elected as a Whig Representative to the Congress of 1843-1845.

Any pleasure he might have had in the event was obscured by another emergency. Caroline suffered a stroke during the campaign and young George, a few weeks later, came down with a virulent case of typhoid fever. Marsh had hoped to go to Washington in the fall to rent a quiet house for his family, instead of having to put up with the lack of privacy in a boarding house, as so many Congressmen did. But young George was in an alarming state, and although Caroline had somewhat recovered, Marsh had so exhausted himself in caring for both sufferers that he, too, fell ill and recovered just in time for the opening of the session. To his sister-in-law he wrote in December, ". . . we left Whitehall at 12 o'clock, Tuesday, arrived at Glen's Falls about 5:00 p.m., where we spent the night. Yesterday we went on to Saratoga, and today we reached Albany at 1½ p.m. George bore the journey very well, and though he cannot yet walk, he evidently is gaining strength. I brought him in my arms the whole way. . . ."

Earliest known photograph of the White House, a daguerrotype taken in 1847. LOC

THE weary little party arrived in Washington after a long trip by steamer and train in a muddy, wintry city, only to find all the houses already let, and had to accept what makeshift arrangements offered. A boarding house that doubled as a hotel, and was kept by the brother of President Tyler was the best they could find. They shared the premises with fifty others, almost equally divided between Northerners and Southerners.

Marsh complained that he was weak and lame, "sadly dispirited about my family . . . and I ought to be in bed, but I keep about and am trying to learn my trade as well as I can. Every step I have taken has been met by some disappointment that has thwarted every calculation I made."

The Vermonters already knew that animosity between North and South was building up in the nation. Marsh abhorred slavery, but thought the South was not altogether to blame as long as the letter of the Constitution upheld slave-holding rights. He hoped that the curse of slavery could be eliminated without destroying the Union. "Slavery is on the defensive . . . slaveholders find themselves overborne by the force of public opinion through the civilized world." Not entertaining any hostility toward Southerners, Marsh was surprised to find to what pitch feelings had risen in the capital. Caroline related how "The first morning after his arrival at his lodgings, Mr. Marsh found himself seated at the breakfast table with a colleague from New England on his right hand, an old Vermont friend on his left, and three Southern gentlemen opposite, one of whom was a young gentleman from Baltimore . . . This young man was looking over a newspaper and commenting aloud on various paragraphs, sometimes to one of the gentlemen by him, and sometimes audibly soliloquizing, all evidently for the benefit of those sitting opposite him. It would be difficult to imagine language more insulting to the North than that used by the young Baltimorean." The Northerners of both sexes held their tongues until they met upstairs with the landlord, who apologized, assuring them that it would not happen again. But Caroline said that the atmosphere at the dining table remained charged with ill feeling the whole winter.

Sure that such a setting for their life in Washington would not be tolerable for another winter, the Marshes found a little house in the west end, between 19th and 20th Streets on the south side of F Street. The new Congressman could enjoyably walk the two miles to and from the capitol. The walk, he said, spared him the nuisance of dealing with office seekers and reporters. The mild winters and early springs, beautiful and flowery, gave him the chance for delightful early morning or evening walks with his family or friends. And Caroline, invalid though she was, enjoyed playing hostess to an ever-increasing group of friends. The Marsh's selection of wine was excellent, one acquaintance said, but their house was a bit cramped. A number of old cronies were in town, Rufus Choate for one, Marsh's best friend at Dartmouth, and Congressman, later Senator and Postmaster-General, Jacob Collamer, whom Marsh had known as a boy in Woodstock. With the crusty, old ex-President John Quincy Adams, Marsh served on a number of committees, and found himself in agreement about style and politics. Webster he respected as he did Clay, but his dislike of popular enthusiams kept him at a distance. "The boat is just in with Mr. Clay on board, and

Washington, looking east on F Street, as it was in Marsh's time. NYPL

thereupon a great shouting, throwing up of caps, and blowing of brazen instruments. Mr. Clay is to remain until tomorrow night, unless the shakers demolish him before that time. I think I'll save him one shake by keeping out of his reach. I hate man-worship in all shapes."

There was another reason for wishing to move to private quarters. "George is in better health . . . but . . . the influence of the servant boys about the hotel is bad and, of course, we cannot confine the child entirely to our own rooms."

Marsh's relations with his son were never easy. Devotedly nursing the boy through numerous childhood illnesses, he was too ready to be critical of the boy's lively outspokenness. George, said his father, "had

Above: Rufus Choate. UVM, *Below: Jacob Collamer.* VHS

the faults of an only child, and a delicate one at that." He considered the boy disrespectful when he offered advice to his father about financial affairs. Though intelligent and quick-witted, George never did well at school. "He has learned a good deal of German, and speaks it with considerable fluency, though he hath a contempt for the superstitious observance of rules touching genders and cases, but so far as I can discover has made very little progress in anything else. . . ." One can only feel sympathy with George, the son of a man who knew twenty languages. With children other than his own son, Marsh was a loving, warm companion, treating them as equals. Caroline paints a charming

picture of the grave, preoccupied man walking down F Street towards the capital as ". . . little feet hurried after him and a little hand laid in his with touching confidence."

In his relations with bright young men Marsh showed his affectionate and witty nature. The presence of two young women, Caroline's sister and Harriet's niece, attracted a swarm of young males to the house on F Street. Marsh, at first intimidating with his piercing look and imposing frame, was soon found to have a ready and sympathetic smile beneath the vast beard, which now spread out impressively over his face and chest.

He encouraged young artists to make his house an agreeable resort in which they could study the engravings he had brought down from Burlington. One of the young unknowns was Eastman Johnson, who made crayon portraits of Marsh and the family, and later became well-known for his portraits of famous men. But it was in the diplomatic and scientific circles that the Marshes made the friends they enjoyed the most. George's linguistic abilities, his wide interests, and Caroline's literary pursuits made them welcome among the famous and interesting not only in Washington, but in the East. The British Minister was happy to visit them in Burlington during the summer recess, and in their journeys to and from Vermont, the Marshes would often stop off in Boston to see Louis Agassiz, the geologist, or George Ticknor, the eminent authority on the Romance languages. With Colonel and Mrs. James Estcourt, the British Commissioner to settle the boundary dispute between the United States and Canada, the Marshes became lifelong friends. The Estcourts accepted the Marshes' invitation to spend some weeks in Vermont, though Caroline was worried that the little house might prove to be too cramped. But it all worked out very well. During that terribly hot summer the guests were whisked off to the cool brick library, separate from the house, to spend the morning looking at the host's books and engravings; at noon they ate a picnic lunch among the tomes. After a walk or drive before dinner, a pleasant evening followed on the shady porch, while Mrs. Estcourt sketched. Caroline said that Marsh never again gave himself such an extended holiday as this.

Another couple with whom they were intimate were the Bairds. Marsh had known Mary Churchill Baird since her childhood, she being the daughter of General Sylvester Churchill of Woodstock, and a talkative, bright girl, who "never laid any claim to beauty." Young Spencer Baird, later to be an authority on the vertebrates of North America, had as a 15-year-old boy been given a collection of birds by Audubon. By the time he was 27, his zoological collection had grown to include more than 3,000 birds, in addition to reptiles, skulls, and skeletons. He ap-

Opposite: Marsh's good friend, Col. James Estcourt, became a Major General during the Crimean War. He poses, center, with his headquarters staff. DL
Right: Spencer Baird, the second Secretary of the Smithsonian Institute, married Mary Churchill, of Woodstock. SI

The Nation's Capitol, a daguerrotype taken around 1850, before the present dome was added. LOC

proached Marsh when seeking a position as a curator at the Smithsonian, and through Marsh's influence was eventually appointed Assistant Secretary of the Institution. Spencer Baird and his wife were the recipients of Marsh's most amusing and witty letters, evoking, in turn, Baird's teasing about Marsh's terrible handwriting. Did Marsh call Mary a "pious fisherwoman" or a "precious penwoman," and couldn't Marsh sharpen his quill pen? Caroline and George came to regard the Bairds virtually as their own children. All in all, the climate of Washington, for both sociability and weather, was so salubrious that the once retiring Marsh was often seen to enjoy himself at teas, receptions, and even some of Washington's many balls!

All the while, Marsh worked hard at Congressional duties. Deadly dull though most of the sessions and committee meetings were, he never missed any, and in this regard again proved an exception to the rule. His constituents found that their letters were answered faithfully the day they were received, and in the hand of George P. Marsh, himself, for the daily stipend of eight dollars did not permit hiring secretaries. "My correspondents are very numerous," he bewailed, "the day that I do not receive ten letters requiring replies is an easy one." Still, by judicious napping in the House, he was able to keep up his late night attendance and maintain his 5:00 a.m. rising. During the morning session, after answering letters, he would scan the roll to see who would be speaking; then, satisfied that he would miss nothing important, he went quietly to sleep. Caroline said it became a game with the balcony watchers to bet which of the two, Marsh or John Quincy Adams, would drop off first.

With the Democrats in control, Marsh as a Whig thought of his proper role as obstructionist to fight for tariffs on behalf of Northern manufacturers, to abolish slavery, and to prevent the annexation of Texas, which would only add to the Democrats' power. All of these efforts failed.

He made a major speech pleading for high tariffs in 1844. "Myself a manufacturer, I know too well the indispensable necessity of estimating profit and loss in advance. There is scarcely a woolen factory in New England which has not lost a sum equal to its entire capital, since 1837." "Free trade," he added, "was an unholy combination between our own government and the capitalists of Europe."

Tempers sometimes ran high on the floor of the House of Representatives. NYPL

On the annexation of Texas he felt strongly. Texas had been a republic nine years when the United States offered it statehood in 1845. Henry Clay, the head of Marsh's party, had fought annexation and was thoroughly trounced for the presidency by James Polk. The morning after the election, Marsh, in an unusually excited manner, pointed out the window, "Do you know what that flag is waving over? There is the slave market of Washington . . . and that flag means Texas, and Texas means civil war before we have done with it." What good would the annexing of Texas do? Would it promote emancipation in the Northern slave-holding states? Or aid American commerce and increase Northern manufactures? The answer was "no". He knew nothing so unlikely to increase strength and prosperity as the Republic of Texas.

The Mexican War that ensued he called "unjust," and any treaty "humiliating" to Mexico and "shameful" to the United States. "There is no present necessity of extension for the accommodation of our growing population. . . ." he said in the debate on annexing Mexico's former territories. "But what evidence is there that the possession of New Mexico or California, however permanent, can be attended with any

John Quincy Adams, an 1843 daguerrotype. MMA

A Brady portrait of Marsh, before leaving for Turkey. LOC

solid advantages to the people of this country? They are separated from us by sterile and arid deserts, or chains of lofty and almost impassable mountains. . . . Above all, they are inhabited by a mixed population, of habits, opinions, and characters incapable of sympathy or assimilation with our own, a race whom the experience of an entire generation has proved to be unfitted for self-government and unprepared to appreciate, sustain or enjoy free institutions."

Marsh was not only shortsighted in his failure to see the need for more land room, he cast doubt on the ability of technology, the technology that he had praised in his speech at Burlington to make the deserts habitable, to span the distances between East and West. Above all, he appeared to fear that the "mixed population" would contaminate the freedom-loving descendants of the Goths. Years later he said, "I was fully convinced of the truth of my position then. . . . I can see that there is another side to the question." George Marsh was never afraid of being inconsistent. When reminded that an opinion differed from another he had held, he calmly replied, "Very likely. A man who cares for truth can't afford to care for consistency." Marsh remained too aloof, too reluctant to be on backslapping terms with his fellow Congressmen, to be a really effective politician. Caroline had made of him a more genial person, but he took the tricky machinations of politics as an affront.

His greatest achievements were not on the House floor, but in committee. He was a member of the House Foreign Relations Committee and of the Smithsonian Committee, assignments that exercised to the full his capacity for hard work. "There isn't any Christmas vacation for us poor dogs nowadays. Our mill goes, whether there is any water or no. We . . . work like horses."

In 1835 President Jackson announced that a wealthy English chemist had left $500,000 to the federal government. James Smithson, the illegitimate son of the Duke of Northumberland, having felt rejected by his father's country, spent his life abroad in the company of learned men of science. On his death he left his entire estate to the United States of America to found at Washington, under the name of the Smithsonian Institution, an establishment for the "increase and

James Smithson as an elegant Oxford student. SI
His unexpected bequest established the United States Smithsonian Institute, seen opposite, in 1865. LOC

diffusion of knowledge among men." Smithson left his fortune to the United States perhaps because he wished to perpetuate his name in a country that overlooked the circumstances of a man's birth.

At that time $500,000 was an enormous sum, the allocation of which was a tremendous responsibility. At once, factions arose in dispute over the disposal of the money. Should it be spent to house the mouldering, long-stored specimens brought back by Lewis and Clark and the Pike Expeditions? Jefferson Davis wanted a perpetual series of popular lectures, Rufus Choate a library, Andrew Johnson normal schools, John Quincy Adams an observatory. By 1844 two opposing groups had formed: practical men who wanted agricultural schools, and intellectuals like Marsh and Adams who wanted a national museum and a research library.

Marsh's longest and most effective speech in Congress was a plea in favor of the library ". . . one of the best speeches ever delivered in the House," said Adams. The Hough-Marsh Bill proposed to honor Smithson's bequest for the increase in knowledge "by collecting specimens . . . by gathering objects in every branch of industrial, decorative and imaginative art. It proposes to define the knowledge . . . by throw-

ing open to public uses the diversified collection of the Institution in every branch of human inquiry . . . ." The library envisioned by Marsh did not materialize, though lately elements of it have been incorporated. But the Smithsonian quickly became, as he had hoped, a center for original research and a clearing house in almost every field of scientific endeavor. Marsh started the exchange of specimens and pamphlets which, carried on and enlarged by Spencer Baird, made the Smithsonian the great institution it now is.

Disappointment met him yet again on his summer return to Burlington in 1846. Caroline had not benefited from her stay in Washing-

A disastrous fire destroyed the Smithsonian and Marsh's collection of engravings in 1865. From Harper's Weekly. SI

ton as they had hoped. In desperation Marsh wrote to Dr. Hayes, in Philadelphia, that the cold salt water showers had had some effect. Would it not hasten matters if Caroline left off the oil-cloth cap and let the water fall directly on her head?

The situation at the mill was desperate. With the South in control of Congress, it was folly to keep the mill in operation; the buildings and machinery were disposed of in a ruinous sale. Almost all the capital invested was lost; the land around it was much depreciated. But Marsh's main regret was that now he would have no money to buy more engravings for his collection.

Marsh had enjoyed his two terms in Congress; he felt he had been of use in the committees he had been assigned to, while doing his best for the Whig cause by fighting "Annexation." He had worked to keep Vermont in the camp of the Whig candidate, Taylor. He had stumped tirelessly, he wrote to Mrs. Estcourt, making "two, sometimes three speeches a day, of from one and a half to three hours in length, at points from ten to thirty miles distant. . . ."

When Taylor was safely in the White House, Marsh spoke to his friends about his desire for a diplomatic post in Europe. He was convinced now that that was his only chance to get ahead. Perhaps in a different climate Caroline's health would improve. "Personally I do not know that I have anything at stake in the late presidential election, though some of my friends . . . think it possible I may be sent abroad in a diplomatic capacity. At any rate I have had a puff in a Boston paper recommending me as a Minister at Berlin on the grounds that I 'can speak German like a brick.' " He and Caroline were pleased when several members of the diplomatic corps told the State Department that their governments would be happy to have him accredited to them.

He had hoped for Berlin, but on May 29, 1849, he was at once pleased and chagrined to receive notice of his appointment as Minister in Residence to the Ottoman Empire. "The post to which I am appointed is not what I should have selected nor where I should expect to be most useful." But both must have been happy at the thought of leaving the United States and their financial worries behind.

That summer was a sorely trying one for Marsh. He had to arrange his business affairs so as to have them in some sort of order, and there would be a long interval between his last salary payment as a Congressman and the first after his duties in Turkey had begun. The State Department in those days was not as solicitous about its employees' welfare as it is now. Then he must also shoulder the task of planning his stay abroad and buying the household goods that would be unobtainable in far-off Constantinople. For Caroline was again very ill, too ill to be of help. She had to be left in New York for most of the summer close to her doctors. In addition, Marsh wanted to collect specimens abroad for his young protege, biologist Spencer Baird. What should these be? "Son Baird, what volant, natant or repent thing, of those that fly, swim or creep, over in or around the Bosphorus, do you most desire in pickle? Name the volatile, aquatic, or reptile and it shall be sent to you. . . ." Instruments for observation, casks and tins of spirits had to be found and prepared for shipping. At the same time he had to choose his official party: Caroline, George, the two young ladies, his old friend Caroline Paine, who had become a friend also of Caroline Marsh, and his attaché, young Mr. Lovett.

Money had to be found to pay for the goods and for the passage of his party. Hard-pressed, Marsh decided there was nothing to do but sell his beloved art collection, his superb collection of engravings. It was then an unusual, almost freakish avocation. Among the treasures was a portfolio of Dürer's work, twenty from Dürer's own hand, thirteen different portraits of the artist and a large number of other prints. Claude Lorrain, Rembrandt, Holbein were also represented, as well as the "best and rarest works and folios of drawings by Rembrandt and Da Vinci and many plates by Hogarth and Flaxman." Over the years Marsh had spent more than $4500 for the group of works; he sold it to the Smithsonian Institution for what, even in those days, was a paltry $3,000. He must many times have regretted his decision to sell, for after the Smithsonian burned down in 1865 Charles Sumner wrote Marsh that most of the choice prints had been destroyed. Those that had escaped were scattered about in a fashion that showed the collection had been badly used. The sale moreover hardly helped Marsh in his need, for the thrifty institution delayed payment for five years.

It was this type of sailing ship which carried Marsh to France. PMS

Marsh was miserable at sea. Quarters were cramped and seasickness was his constant and unwelcome condition. *Both* NYPL

THE little party set off from New York on the 21st of September, 1849, with what must have been mountains of luggage. Though the days of steam had begun, Marsh chose a sailing packet at the strong suggestion of Caroline's doctors. For a whole miserable month, on the interminable voyage to France against head winds, Marsh was seasick. "Ocean in all its phases is an uninviting object," he wrote to a friend. "I hate the sea and would be well content to pay my share of the cost of filling it up altogether and building good carriagable roads instead." He wrote to his mother from Le Havre that the three Marshes had been seasick for 27 days, but now at an inn they were "feasting on grapes and *fresh* bread and butter!" With what excitement they took the train to Paris, dashing from side to side of the railway carriage, exclaiming over the pollarded willows and the thatched cottages! Caroline said that nothing her husband afterwards saw gave him more pleasure than his first day's glimpse of France.

To the American art collector, Paris was like heaven. "Since our arrival here 3 days ago, I have spent my spare time principally in the Louvre. . . . Mrs. Marsh, unhappily, is thus far little benefited by the voyage, and being unable to stand or walk, has seen nothing as yet." But her resourceful husband persuaded the officials of the museum to open the doors especially for his party. With Caroline in his arms, he climbed innumerable flights of stairs to a waiting wheelchair and, rolled through the empty galleries, she saw all the famed treasures.

The trip through France to Marseilles was not so pleasant. The carriages were broken-down, the river steamers were filthy, the sights were interesting, but the conditions fatiguing. At Marseilles the ship was so cramped and dirty that Marsh and his party chose instead to drive east along the Riviera and across Italy to Naples, Caroline reclining in a portable bed.

One of the earliest-known outdoor views of Paris, a rare and hitherto unpublished daguerrotype of the Pont Neuf. Below: The empty galleries of the Louvre, as Caroline saw them from her wheel chair. Both PL

Before railroads came into common usage, the horse-drawn diligence was a favored mode of travel. LLA

Forty years later Caroline remembered the journey as "an almost uninterrupted succession of pleasurable excitements." Marsh must have been at his most relaxed, far from the worries of his entangled affairs. "The contretemps inseparable from traveling were met by Mr. Marsh with such perfect good humor that there were no scenes with hotel keepers or vetturinos, no disputes with guides or porters. . . . His patience in answering the questions of his traveling companions was inexhaustible, and they were in a constant state of surprise at his seeing a thousand things unnoticed by them until he pointed them out." Though the season was winter the tree-enthusiast Marsh maintained that the display of evergreens, olives, cork trees, cypresses, and umbrella pines could be seen to the best advantage, free of the screen of summer foliage. On to Florence they drove, seeing there again Marsh's old schoolmate Hiram Powers. It was a joyful reunion, for the two men had not seen each other since boyhood, when the Powers family left the Woodstock hillside farm for Ohio. Now Hiram, America's first notable sculptor, was living in Italy, whence he had sent waves of delectable horror through his native land by exhibiting his *Greek Slave,* a female nude, devoid of any hint of modest drapery.

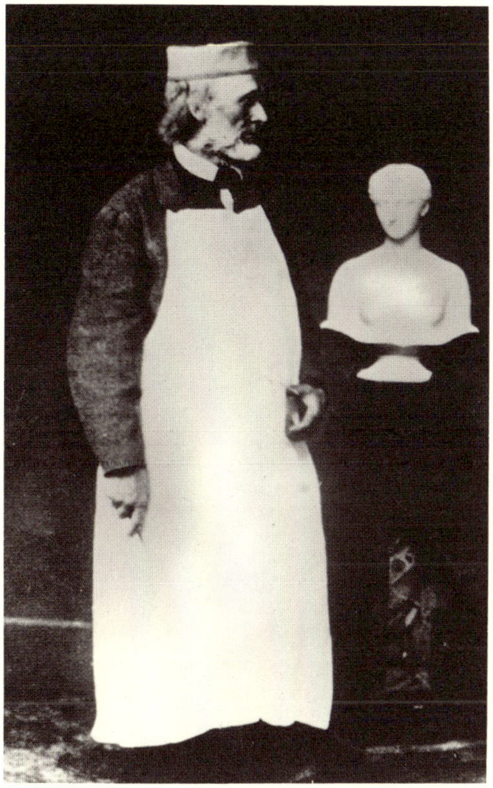

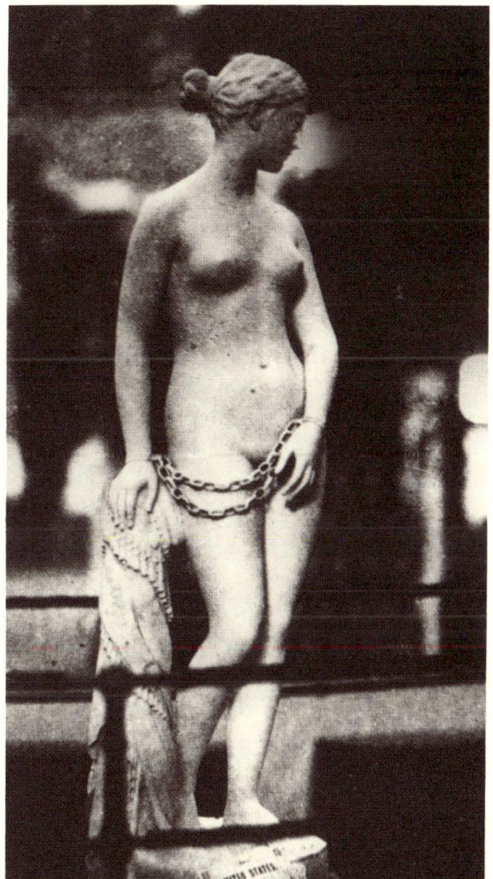

Hiram Powers, the most noted American sculptor of his time, in his Florentine studio. WHS *His totally nude "Greek Slave" caused a furor in Victorian England when it was shown at the Crystal Palace Exhibition in London.* NYHS

When the Marshes arrived at Naples, above, NA, *Vesuvius obligingly put on a spectacular eruption.* NYPL *The party left for Constantinople on the U. S. Frigate Mississippi, seen at lower right.* PMS

In Rome Marsh for the first time saw the ancient city, once the center of an empire, now only a collection of broken columns and gaping palace walls overgrown with vines. He could walk over the buried city and pick up a potsherd that had once been part of a live civilization. In *Man and Nature* he was to use the Roman Empire as an example of what man had done to his environment. When the party arrived in Naples, Vesuvius obligingly put on a spectacular eruption of flaming lava, which Marsh timed as moving at a rate of three feet a minute.

There too, the frigate *U.S. Mississippi* awaited them, and for a peaceful week, they sailed down the Mediterranean, steamed through the Dardenelles, swept around Seraglio Point, and beheld Constantinople, the romantic city of Islamic domes and minarets, glittering in the sunrise.

Alas for romance. The weather changed abruptly, wet snow fell on the voyagers disembarking upon the cobbled-stone pavements inches deep in mud. The horses struggled to pull the passengers and their

luggage up the steep hill to the hotel, but could not do it. All except Caroline got out and pushed the vehicles the rest of the way.

The rooms were huge, dirty, and unheated; the privy was out of order. Finally, Marsh managed to have a smoky brazier brought in, and around this the shivering Americans sat in their overcoats for two miserable weeks until better quarters were found.

Twelve miles away in Therapia, a Greek settlement, a house was rented, perfect for the first summer they spent in Turkey. Caroline's description of it still evokes the almost sensuous pleasure the Vermonters experienced in the mild climate of the Near East. The front of the villa hung over the quay, a broad hall ran through to the rear and opened out on to a succession of terraces, where roses contrasted in hue with cypresses. There they sat and read in the evenings, breathing in the soft, sweet air. The only drawback to the house, besides its being unfit for winter, was the porter who, to show his utter devotion, tried to clasp Marsh reverently about the knees each time the master entered the door. The United States Minister to Turkey was obliged to leap first, skipping nimbly to one side.

Duty in Turkey was on the whole undemanding, for America's relations with that country were relatively uncomplicated. Yet Marsh's lowly diplomatic standing, twenty-seventh on the list, was no handicap to social life; his reputation as a scholar had preceded him. The Marshes were a welcome addition to the international group. Sir Stafford and Lady Canning, Dean of the Corps, were happy to befriend the interesting Americans.

Soon after Marsh had settled in, he was summoned with all the other foreign diplomats to an audience with the Sultan. Abdul Medjed "received us standing before a plain sofa at the upper end of the room, and we took our places in a semicircle around him. . . . My place happened to be at the crown of the arch, just opposite His Majesty, and my Persian friend being next to me. . . . The Persian wore a pelisse of light-figured silk over a tunic of the same material with the trousers and a fine shawl about his waist. He wore neither sword nor dagger and his only ornament was a diamond decoration. A conical cap of black lambskin two feet high, which he did not take off even in the presence, completed his costume, and as he is a tall man of good figure and a fine (dyed) black beard, I thought him as imposing a personage as the best of us. The Sultan wore the fez . . . a frock coat of dark blue cloth bordered with a narrow gold embroidery and loose white pantaloons. . . . The decoration suspended to his neck was the richest assemblage of gems I have ever seen and the centre stone is, I suppose, among the half dozen finest diamonds in the world." In Marsh's words one detects his sense

Constantinople, the romantic city of domes and minarets. NA

Principal entrance to the Old Palace Bab Seadet. PL
Here Marsh attended a diplomatic audience with the Sultan Abdul Medjid, right. AC
Opposite: fiery Hungarian patriot, Ladjos Kossuth, refugee in Constantinople, made life difficult for Marsh. LOC

of amazement that he, George P. Marsh, of Burlington, Vermont, should be present at such a ceremony. One can see how incongruous the tall solid black-frocked figure must have appeared amidst the peacock splendor of the other dignitaries. The Sultan, he reported, was an amiable young man, with liberal notions but was, Marsh feared, inadequate to the task of propping up a nation trembling on the brink of disaster. Turkey, he said, was in a shocking state. "It is a house of cards, and the smallest power in Europe could overthrow it. . . ." His prediction was amply fulfilled in the outbreak of the Crimean War in 1853, when France and Great Britain declared war on Russia in an attempt to keep the Great Bear out of Turkey.

Marsh's worst problem was dealing with the thousands of refugees of the 1840's nationalist revolutions. From Germany, Italy, Hungary, they came, when their rebellious attempts at freedom had failed, to Turkey. From one legation to another they circulated, begging for food, money, protection. Marsh's predecessor had issued passports for money; Marsh refused to do so. He was under tremendous pressure from the dynamic Hungarian, Lajos Kossuth, to do something for his followers who, he threatened, were going to starve to death outside the American Ministry. Kossuth, who had for a short time been President of his native Hungary in its brief freedom from the Austrian Empire, was a difficult man to deal with; his temper had not improved when the republic was crushed and he, too, was forced to flee to Turkey. At first Marsh was wholly in sympathy with the egotistic Hungarian and promised help. The State Department, indeed, instructed him to do so, but

Congress neglected to provide Marsh with the wherewithal. Kossuth refused to listen to Marsh's explanations, and, in order to keep him quiet, the desperate Marsh gave him what he could out of his own pockets. When at last, thanks to Marsh's negotiations, Kossuth and fifty of his followers were given passage on a ship to the United States, he berated the American for being so stingy and uncooperative.

Lack of money was, as always, Marsh's chief problem. He was aghast to find living in Turkey so dear. The niggardly salary of a Minister was manifestly inadequate. The British Ambassador received $60,000, Marsh only $6,000. "I have given no entertainment of any sort, incurred none but the necessary expenses, and yet my household expenditures have exceeded my salary." How could he be expected to promote trade, help starving refugees, influence Turkish officials with expensive presents, he complained in his letters. "The Turks are rude people and measure the consequence of foreigners by the style they live in." President Taylor had been moved by Marsh's pleas, and was about to promote him to Minister Plenipotentiary when Taylor's sudden death put a stop to Marsh's hopes. Vice-President Fillmore was no friend of Marsh's and, in addition, Horace Greeley, whom Marsh had antagonized while both were Congressmen, mounted a vicious newspaper campaign against Marsh. "If Mr. Marsh is sick of it, let him drop off and some good man will be found to take his place for the $6,000." Far away in Constantinople, Marsh could only say, "Greeley's an old, and so far as I know, unprovoked enemy of mine and no new evidence of his malice toward me can surprise me." But in Washington, Vermont

Horace Greeley, publisher of the New York Tribune. Marsh wrote, "Greeley's an old . . . unprovoked enemy of mine." LOC

"The general aspect of Cairo is infinitely more oriental than that of Constantinople." LOC

friends like Solomon Foot were willing to petition the ailing Secretary of State, Daniel Webster, in Marsh's behalf. Foot reported that "Mr. Webster was willing to consider it, but the old man was very gruff . . . and was as ill-mannered as he was ill-natured." Old and cantankerous, Webster died soon after this.

Now winter was coming on, a season that in Turkey is raw and damp. With its thin wooden walls and lack of stoves, the charming house at Therapia was utterly inadequate in cold weather. City houses were much too expensive. There was only one thing to do: leave Constantinople for the winter and travel to Egypt and the Holy Land. Luckily, Webster had earlier agreed that it was fitting for the American Minister to see the other provinces of Turkey.

The group set off in January, and once Marsh had fully recovered from the trip down the Mediterranean, he was like a boy on a holiday from school. "I enjoy new scenes and new people as keenly as I could have done at 20." Everything interested him, shrubs, lizards, costumes, rocks; everything stimulated his powers of observation. "The general aspect of Cairo is infinitely more Oriental than that of Constantinople. The costumes are Eastern, the vegetation, the native houses, the troops

Francis Frith, traveller and early photographer, took this picture of the Emeer Akhoor Mosque in Cairo in 1852. PL

of camels and asses, the strange birds, the water carriers, the women with babies astride their shoulder . . . all belong to another world than ours. . . ." His letters are filled with his exuberant good spirits. "The view from the platform of Gizeh, of Sakkara, and Dashur, and the desert threatening to engulf with its moving sands is one of the finest I have ever seen."

As did all travelers to Egypt, the Marsh party embarked on an almost obligatory voyage up the Nile. "We have a good boat, most excellent servants, dragoman and crew, and I have nowhere enjoyed so many of the pleasures, alloyed with so few of the ordinary discomforts of traveling as in this visit to the Nile."

It was a smooth, restful trip of three months on the river, in a comfortable, broadbeamed dahabieh, powered by two immense lateen sails. Marsh sunned himself on the deck, and watched the banks, green with palms and mimosa, dotted with crocodiles crouching on sandbanks, while Caroline played with a baby ostrich. In the evenings before the fireplace, they ate marvelous meals prepared by their cook from the goods bought every day in the native markets. Hammocks and bunks were everybody's beds, and sleep proved easy in the cool desert night.

As diplomatic voyagers they were much in demand, and on one occasion in Nubia had to make a trip inland to partake of lunch with a village sheikh. "Our parade was a curious one," wrote Caroline, "and most devoutly did I wish that our friends in America could have one glance at us. Mr. Marsh was mounted on a donkey so small that with difficulty he could keep his feet from the ground, one man walked at his side, and another followed behind urging on the poor beast with a sharp stick, and when he broke into a trot, seizing him by the tail to keep up with him more easily. George followed in the same state, and each of

In Cairo, Shepherd's Hotel was the gathering place for the international set. NYPL

114

All tourists climbed, or tried to climb the Great Pyramid, seen in detail, left, GEH, *and from the desert, below.* LOC
Right: The "shadouf" had been used to draw water from the Nile for thousands of years. AMMH
Below: In such a dahabieh as this the Marshes travelled the Nile in style. LLA

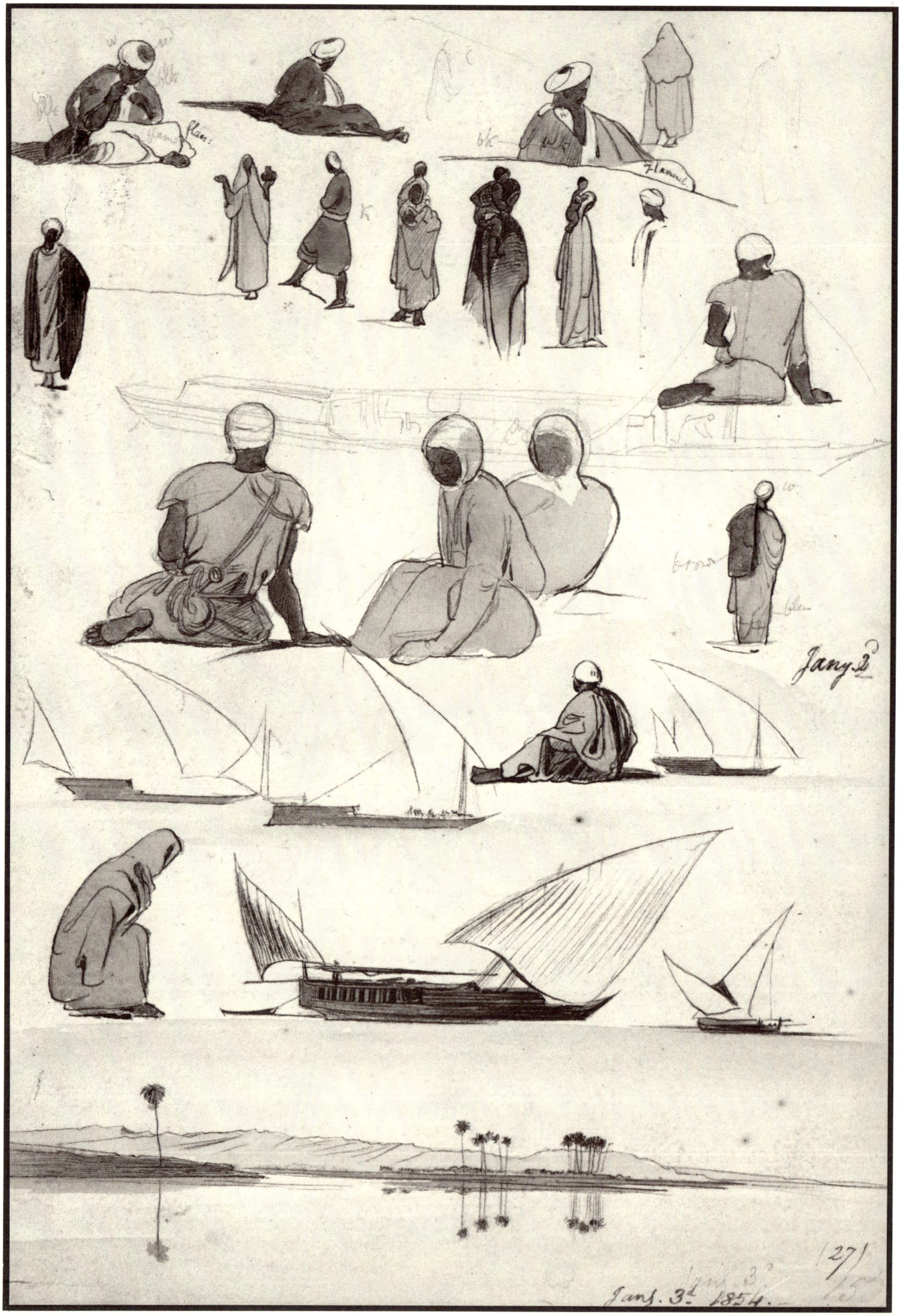

Jany 3d
(27)
Jany. 3d 1854.

the demoiselles had a similar mounture, and were similarly attended. I followed in my litter, carried by four of our sailor boys, while Serour, the old black pilot, walked in solemn silence by my side, holding an umbrella over my head. A troop of inhabitant men and women and children brought up the rear."

Page from one of Edward Lear's sketchbooks. The noted landscape painter and nonsense poet travelled in Egypt soon after the Marshes were there. AC
Right: The lovely island of Philae, near Aswan, now flooded by the dam. LOC

To their embarrassment, Caroline was given a full-grown ostrich to replace the baby, who had died from eating too many stones and rubble. The bird, taller than Marsh, was too big to house on the crowded dahabieh. He had to hire a man in a small boat to row it behind them, hoping to be able to sell the great bird in Cairo, and not hurt the feelings of the giver.

Crippled though she was, Caroline was determined not to be left out of any sightseeing. In her diary she tells how, at the temple of Esna, "We scrambled up the steep bank as best we could, those on foot getting along tolerably well, but for the lame who had to go on donkey back, it was not so easy. A man walked on each side of us, a third dragged the poor beast by the nose, and a fourth pushed from behind. With an abundance of screaming and shouting, we found ourselves at last on top of the bank, and in a very few minutes stood within a splendid temple."

In Luxor they were ensconsed in a house built on the roof of the huge temple, its doors painted mummy cases. "The late occupants," wrote Marsh, "stripped of their cerements, are ranged in a row against the courtyard wall facing us."

The only disappointment for Marsh was the spoilage of the specimens he had collected for Spencer Baird. Ouzo was the only spirit available and the asp, the lizards, two pelicans' heads, beetles, frogs and some fish had all spoiled. He hoped to go back to Egypt next winter,

Half-buried, the massive pillars of Karnak emerge from the sands, LOC, *and opposite, Ramses II gazes over his desert kingdom at Abu Simbal, calmly ignoring the graffiti of later visitors.* AMNH

even to Khartoum, and wanted Baird to be sure and send at once, for mail was so slow, not only spirits but vessels, glass if possible, for casks dried out too fast in that arid climate. "I shall look out sharp for salamanders and if I find a new one, you shall name it Salamandrilus Bairdii or the like."

They had their hearts set on a forty day trip taking the path of the ancient Israelites out of Egypt, across the Sinai to the Red Sea. Marsh wanted to see Petra, Jordan's Red City of the Dead. From there they would strike out for the Wadi el Arabia, the path to the Dead Sea and rest under the trees of Hebron before proceeding to Bethlehem and Jerusalem. Caroline, who could walk only a few steps without faintness, never flinched from a journey that even today with motorized vehicles is arduous. They set off from Cairo with thirty camels, all but Caroline riding astride. She was crunched into an extremely uncomfortable "mahafa," a box five by two feet, with a cover, hanging on one side of the beast, while trunks on the other served as counterpoise.

For a landscape enthusiast such as Marsh, this country was the most exciting he had ever seen. Jotting notes on his knees as his camel shuffled along, he wrote, "I have never seen any natural scenery so sublime . . . so wildly beautiful . . . the precipices are often truly stupendous. In passing from one wadi to another, one skirts the base of such precipices, gradually ascending till near the head of the ravine. Then you begin to climb the side by paths so narrow, rough and steep that one who had never seen a camel ascend them would say they were wholly impracticable for any beast of burden. There is often not the least appearance of a track, and the camel climbs from rock to rock like a mountain goat. . . . The dangers of these passes are not so very formid-

Hill town in Palestine; stone-walled terraces retain precious soil and water. LLA

able to travellers in health, because the camel, with so light a burden as a single person, is so sure-footed that accidents are almost unheard of, and besides, the rider, if he prefers it, can walk where he thinks his own feet safer than those of his beast. But with C. the case was far otherwise. The camel that carried her, though a very large and strong animal (seven feet, three inches high), was heavily burdened with the mahafa and its contents, and the width of this mahafa was a great obstacle in the very narrow passages. . . . While walking over such perilous places behind her camel . . . I was often obliged to shut my eyes until the most dangerous points were passed. . . ." His admiration for Caroline's staunch bearing glows in a letter to his mother. "She has shown as much courage in facing dangers as she has manifested fortitude in enduring suffering and has met pains and hazards of a very trying climate without ever exhibiting a token of weakness or terror."

For one so prone to seasickness, it was curious that Marsh fell in love with the ungainly camel. Far from being uncomfortable on their backs, he boasted that he could write notes, and even take a sighting from the saddle. He wrote, ". . . sidewise or backwards with legs crossed or dangling and arms folded or akimbo, with no fear your beast will kick

Barren Palestinian hills show the results of centuries of overgrazing. LOC

Desert travellers, such as the Marshes, were tented in comfort and style. HSM, *and below,* LOC
Opposite: Marsh particularly wanted to see Petra, Jordan's Red City of the Dead. HSM

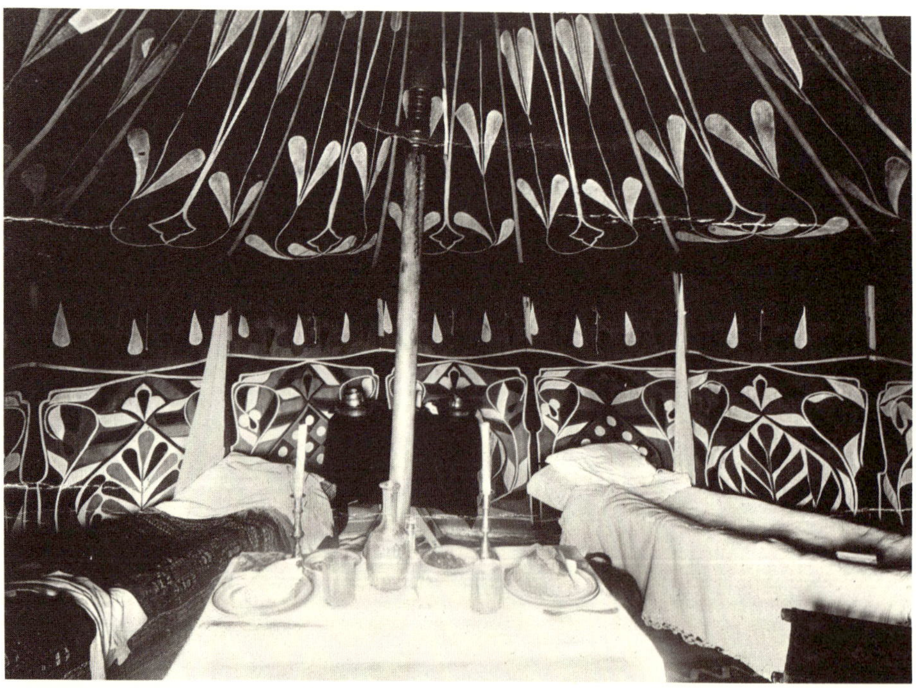

up or stumble and pitch you over his head or rear and throw you over his tail at the sight of an old woman or take the bit in his teeth and run to Quoddy with you."

Their days began at two in the morning and went on, sometimes in temperatures hovering around 110 degrees, for nine or ten hours without a stop. They had an abundance of tents, folding chairs and supplies, including a milk camel brought along by a sheikh who, attracted by Caroline, carried a pint of fresh milk to her at every halt.

Marsh was in top form, fascinated by everything he saw in the alien climate. He wrote to his mother, "It is very difficult to convey an adequate idea of the peninsular desert. One who has lived, as you have done, among mountains covered with verdure may easily imagine them stripped of all vegetation, jagged peaks, bare precipices, bald rock, etc., but the colors of the mountains of Arabia cannot be imagined . . . they must be seen . . . ."

All had gone well thus far, although Marsh was disappointed in the buoyancy of the Dead Sea when he floated on its surface. After resting in Hebron the party bade farewell to their camels, mounted mules and went on to Bethlehem and Jerusalem. Then bad luck seemed to follow the party. In Bethlehem Caroline had a touch of fever and in Jerusalem young George fell ill. Nevertheless they pushed on with the long

exhausting journey to Nazareth where Marsh, tired by nursing, came down with a dangerously high fever. The only available help, an old Spanish priest, tried to cure it by bleeding. When Marsh stopped breathing the agitated priest poured ammonia over his face, arousing Marsh, but scalding him severely. A week's rest at Mt. Carmel enabled them to mount their mules once more but by the time they had reached Magdal on the Sea of Galilee both the Marshes were seriously ill. They might have died in that low, unhealthy spot but for the fortunate arrival of missionary John Bowen, who persuaded the local Arabs to build litters and carry them to higher, cooler hills. There they recovered enough to be moved in their litters to Damascus and Beirut.

Jerusalem was the ultimate destination of all travellers to the Holy Land. Opposite: A view of The Garden of Gethsemane and the Mount of Olives. AC
Right: The Damascus Gate, LOC *and below, street leading to Herod's Palace.* HSM

Caroline was still very ill when they got back to Constantinople to find that they had been given up for dead. While the trip had been physically debilitating, they both agreed they couldn't wait to get back to Egypt and the desert. It had been a fruitful time for Marsh. He had taken compass bearings, registered rainfall and temperatures, measured stream widths, estimated wind velocities. He had sent back to the Smithsonian cobra heads, fishes, bats, scorpions and lizards, always worrying that the containers would leak the spirits and the specimens would rot. But more valuable than all of the measurements and pickled fish was the perception he got of man's action on the land. "The very earth, the naked rocks and sands of the desert . . . the meadows levelled and the hills rounded . . . by this assiduous husbandry of hundreds and hundreds of generations. . . ." He had seen in the barren hills and eroded streambeds of Vermont the immediate consequences of man's careless abuse of the land, but in the Near East were the ultimate and centuries-long results of the same processes. The scenery of Egypt and the Arabian Desert confirmed what he had learned as a boy in Vermont.

They were glad to be back in Constantinople for Caroline's sake, but in the accumulated mail was unwelcome news. Marsh's financial affairs in Vermont were in a perilous state. The proposed return to Egypt now might never materialize. Thoroughly disheartened, Marsh came down with erysipelas and jaundice, but soon recovered.

The River Jordan and the Promised Land from the Cliffs of Moab, Palestine. AC
Opposite: The Acropolis, Athens, before it was engulfed by urban sprawl. It was land below the Acropolis over which Jonas King and the Greek government quarreled. PL

They were just resigning themselves to a winter in Therapia, this time well supplied with stoves, when the State Department ordered Marsh to Athens, to disentangle a complex land dispute, involving a cantankerous missionary, Jonas King, over land King owned near the Acropolis. King had, in addition, so antagonized the theocratic government with his Protestant proselytizing that he was threatened with banishment from Greece. It took Marsh six weeks to wade through the mountain of ill-written transcripts, and handle the uncompromising King and the corrupt Greek officials. He concluded that King had been unjustly prosecuted by the priests, urged that the United States Government demand remission of the banishment, and go on to establish the justice of King's land claims.

Until Washington had decided how to deal with Marsh's recommendations, the envoy was unable to return to his post in Turkey. Killing time in Athens was expensive, the city was terribly hot, his eyes felt strained by the long hours of translation, and when a doctor advised a stay at Bad Gleichenberg, Marsh and his party left for Austria. Secretary of State Webster had promised that his expenses would be paid by Congress for his work on the King mission, so for once Marsh need not worry about money.

Taking a ship to Trieste, their route across Austria to the Spa took them through conspicuously fertile country, and his letters to his brother Charles, farming back home in Woodstock, were full of agricultural interest. "The country between Gratz and Gleichenberg reminds me strongly of Vermont in its natural features, but the care bestowed upon forests presents a marked contrast to our neglect of them." To Baird he wrote, "Seriously it is a shame that I have not the knowledge of nature that every traveller, who goes a Sabbath day's journey from home, ought to have. I see strange stones, plants, animals, geographical formations and gaze vacantly at them, but what availeth it? Well, I'll write a book some day and show that one ignoramus is as good a traveller as any body."

His only regret, he wrote Baird, was that he had not been able to do much collecting in Athens. "It is odd I cannot get salamanders, though I see hundreds of them. I can't catch them, and money won't hire natives to do it. I have tried boys, Croats, Bulgarians, my own servant, but in vain."

But while he was making good use of his enforced holiday in Austria, he wondered about his future. The Democrat Franklin Pierce, who won the election of 1852, was now President, and Marsh's position was in danger: "I tremble at Presidents and such like, Secretaries of State and influential Democrats, and am as uncomfortable as Damocles with the sword suspended over him." He knew that as a Whig his days in Constantinople were numbered. "I dread being turned out and going home where nothing but poverty and mortification await me," he wrote Baird.

His recommendation for the settlement of the King case was adopted with praise, but back in Constantinople the blow fell; he was to be superseded. Marsh was aghast. Meager as the salary of Minister in Residence was, it was better than nothing. "I do not know what I can do at home. I cannot return to the law after so long an interval and I see no other opening." Moreover, the prospect of living the rest of his life in Burlington was not appealing. Where would he find such a stimulating circle as that which included men like Sir Harry Verney, Florence Nightingale's brother-in-law, or the Earl of Carlisle, statesman and writer? Vermont was going to be worse than dull; it would be like going into some dreary hibernation.

Marsh wrote, "Giving up the Alps (would be) like giving up all the material world." LOC

MARSH and company left Turkey on Christmas Day, just as the Crimean War broke out. He was in no hurry to face financial troubles at home and so drew out the return journey for seven months, pleading the perils of a winter crossing and the dangerous effects of a change of climate. In Sicily Mt. Etna favored the travelers with an eruption and Marsh was in his element scrambling about the edge of the smoking lava with the local experts. The Roman spring held them for two months, but as soon as the Alpine passes were open they were forced to trundle Caroline across five-foot snowdrifts in a wheelbarrow.

Crossing an Alpine pass was a hazardous adventure. NYPL

By August they were back in the United States, to find their worst anticipations realized. Burlington, which had abandoned its lake shipping trade for the railroad, was in collapse. The promoters of the Vermont Central Railroad, friends and associates of Marsh, on whom the little city had built its hopes of a golden era after the failure of the woolen mill, had milked the company dry, issued valueless stock, and left no money for repairs. Most of the city's businessmen were bankrupt. Marsh found himself in desperate straits, liable for worthless promissory notes to the tune of $50,000, his precious farmland sliced diagonally in half by the railroad line. His only chance of paying his debts was the compensation he had been promised by the government for his work in settling the case in Athens. "I did not seek the Greek mission. It cost me months of severe labor and considerable pecuniary loss."

He hurried off to Washington to put in his claim before the House and found more trouble. His request met with antagonism and outright hostility. The cause was not hard to find. When he had first come to Constantinople, Marsh had had to reprimand a consular official, one Francis Dainese, and had finally to send him home for "gross and criminal practice." Ever since, Dainese had been hard at work in the capital spreading poisonous lies about Marsh. Unfortunately the lies reached the ears of men who had been antagonized by Marsh in his congressional years and were now only too happy to retaliate by believing them. Marsh, witty and affectionate in his wide circle of friends, could be abrupt and impatient with those he considered fools or knaves, and had no hesitation in letting them know his opinion. Men with long-standing grudges against him had found their chance to strike back.

Marsh was horrified to hear the rumor Dainese had been spreading. It was that far from settling a very difficult case in Athens, Marsh had spent a mere twenty-three days there and had traveled the rest of the year in Europe as a man of leisure at the taxpayers' expense. His old enemy Horace Greeley, of the *Tribune,* crowed happily the news that Marsh's Greek mission was, "little better than an excursion of pleasure." In vain Marsh tried to explain that he had not been able to return to his post until the government had considered his recommendations, that it was as inexpensive to travel as to remain in Athens. Then someone put about the calumny that because Marsh was a well-known anti-catholic, he had sent Catholic Dainese home for that reason. Bedeviled by his creditors in Burlington; Marsh had also to fight off this swarm of lies and innuendoes in Washington; he traveled frantically between the two cities. For six years he battled enmity and apathy in Congress for his money. Only when it finally came into his hands was he able to free himself from his load of debt.

Meanwhile, what could he do? Where could he turn? His brother-in-law and partner, Lyman, had (he thought) betrayed him, or at least stupidly created most of Marsh's troubles, and the greedy friends whom he had trusted had robbed him legally. He felt surrounded by malefactors and nincompoops; he was bankrupt at 55, when most men look forward to comfortable retirement. Desperately depressed, he asked Caroline how she liked being married to a pauper. Always courageous, she rebuked him. "My dear husband, remember that these things assume an apparent magnitude which they really do not possess. Do not give in to self-pity."

With his creditors dogging his heels, Marsh cast about for a way to earn money. The search lasted nearly six years, filled with a variety of absurd offers. A dentist wanted him to act as a travel agent introducing American tourists to European dignitaries. Harvard wanted him to teach history. The Marshes would have loved to live in Cambridge, but he refused reluctantly. His affairs were in such a state that he must devote all his time to them. He would have had no time to compose his notes and prepare his lectures.

It was at this time that he entered on the unsuccessful quarry business. In an era when the craze was for anything made of marble — buildings, fireplaces, mantle ornaments, tabletops, bookends — Marsh hoped that a vein found locally would help to refill his bank account. "Quarrying, which is now the great affair of the nation, goes well. I go down everyday." The marble, shipped to New York, was quickly rejected: it was too hard and brittle to be worked profitably. This was also the time he tried to patent his surveying instruments, only to be told they were out of date.

Dispirited, he refused academic positions. Grumpily, he turned down the provostship of the University of Pennsylvania, "I hate boys, hate tuition, hate forms." He remembered his winter at Norwich University. The truth was, the positions paid too little.

In this dolorous period one cheerful note was struck: his infatuation with the camel. Two years' observation had convinced him that the patient, useful animal might thrive in the deserts of western America, ". . . which in their general character bear a considerable re-

American sailors help a native driver load the unwilling animals. NM

In the American desert, the cavalrymen had great difficulty managing the unfamiliar beasts. NA

semblance to those of Arabia." It could, moreover, serve in a double capacity as beast of burden and instrument of war. "There are few more imposing spectacles than a body of armed men, advancing under the quick pace of the trained dromedary; and this sight, with the ability of the animal to climb ascents impracticable to horses, and thus to transport mountain howitzers, light artillery, stores and other military material into the heart of the mountains, would strike with a salutary terror the Comanches, Lipans and other savage tribes upon our border."

Congress, inspired by a lecture Marsh delivered at the Smithsonian, ordered 74 camels from the Near East, and shipped them to Texas in May, 1856. He hoped to cash in on the interest generated by the arrival of the beasts with a book on the subject. He went thoroughly into the species, breeds, anatomy, and environmental adaptations, diet, training, burden speed and geographical range. "I puff like a bladder," he said, when a subject interested him. The book's very thoroughness was very likely the reason that it sold virtually no copies. The camels themselves fared little better. There were difficulties, of course. As Marsh had warned, the cavalrymen didn't like the way they smelled, riding the beasts made them seasick, horses bolted with fright, and Indians stole them. Nonetheless, they proved themselves as Marsh had thought they would. The army was about to order a thousand more when the Civil War broke out and the remaining animals were left in the desert to shift for themselves. For years thereafter travelers would sometimes see, as if a mirage, the ungainly ghost-like shape of the beasts as they wandered about through the arroyos and draws of the Southwest. A few were rounded up and sold to a circus, but most died in the desert. Only one, Topsy, lived into the twentieth century, dying in 1934 in a Los Angeles zoo. She long outlived Haji Ali, the Arabian camel driver, who had come to the United States with her and her 73 companions. Although the camel experiment had failed, Haji Ali decided he liked the western deserts better than his own and stayed on, becoming the well-liked Hi Jolly to the cowboys. When he died in 1902 his friends in Quartzite, Arizona, built a pyramid over his grave and placed a statue of a camel on top. Thirty-two years later, Topsy's ashes were buried there with those of her driver, Haji Ali.

Plagued as ever by his ailing finances, Marsh now turned in desperation to the lecture platform. It was the golden age of the lecture circuits, for America was bestirring itself, seeking culture. People would listen patiently to almost anyone who had claim to knowledge. Everyone who tried it did well — everyone but Marsh. Caroline explained his failure: "His quiet manner, his rapid utterance, the compact language in which thoughts followed in quick succession — all these were characteristics not likely to draw large audiences." The wry humor he gave vent to in letters and conversations was totally lacking in his dry, fact-filled lectures. Another reason probably was his unwillingness to use the showmanship required for successful platform performance. He dreaded his appearances and put off thinking about them as long as he could.

If the audience were bored by Marsh's talks, he found the people, the scenery, the towns, dreary. "Not all the gophers in Illinois would tempt me to dwell in this famed West," he wrote to Spencer Baird. "I have been in continual peril of my soul . . . by reason of floods, broken bridges, railroad chances and the like, but tomorrow I think I turn my face eastward and I shall bid adieu to the prairies without a sigh." His accommodations were cold and dirty, the food abominable, the trains overcrowded, and never on time, ". . . but while I was expecting the train inside, it went on the outside, carrying my trunks with it so that my Chicago appointment is lost also. The natives I meet in the cars don't know so much as a yellow dog. I am much inclined to return home directly tonight."

Railroad ticket office in the country. The top-hatted figure, center, bears a remarkable resemblance to Marsh. DCL

With all this discomfort, his reward was meager. Often the pay did not cover expenses. The average lecture netted only about fifty dollars. Discouraged, he wrote Caroline., "I shall hang my 'lecturing' on the same peg with my other failures and follies. It must be a long peg and a strong peg to hold them all."

In 1857, when all his efforts to earn a living had failed, another chance as a public servant turned up. The Governor of Vermont appointed him Railroad Commissioner, Fish Commissioner and Statehouse Commissioner — a tribute to his many accomplishments.

Gleefully he set to work to examine the records of the Vermont Central Railroad with a mandate to establish the regulation of rates. "My anathema on the scoundrel railroaders and on all railroads whom I loathe with all my soul!" Already embittered over his lost investments and further inflamed by his recent railroad experiences in the Midwest, he made a very thorough investigation of the Vermont Central and its venal owners. Strangely, for one who espoused the workings of the Industrial Revolution, he recommended government control of transportation and communication services, maintaining that while bureaucracy was a danger it was less evil than private control, which led only to public corruption. Individual selfishness endangered public welfare. This attitude he was to carry over in *Man and Nature* when he spoke of resource conservation. Naturally the Vermont Legislature refused to act on his report. "The Report will probably bring a hornet's nest about my ears, but I shall tell the truth at whatever cost . . . I call the managers rogues. . . ."

As State House Commissioner, Marsh enjoyed himself thoroughly in his role of advising architect. When the State House burned down in 1857, Governor Fletcher appointed Marsh one of three commissioners to see it rebuilt. The other two Vermonters, Norman Williams of Woodstock and John Porter of Hartford, admitted that they had no knowledge of architecture. Only Marsh had acquired a trained eye and informed opinions on the subject, and they gladly deferred to him, ". . . we desire you to exercise your own taste and judgment."

Friendship sprang up between Marsh and the young architect, Thomas Silloway, and Marsh soon found himself an intermediary between Silloway and the choleric Dr. Powers, another Woodstockian,

Opposite page: Marsh's investments in the Vermont Central Railroad, proved as disastrous as this dreadful accident near St. Albans, Vermont. VHS
Right: an early photograph of Vermont's second State House in Montpelier, before 1857, the year in which it was destroyed by fire. VHS
Marsh, as State House Commissioner, persuaded the architect to keep the handsome Doric facade of the old House and add a simple high dome to the third and present State House. Bare hills in the background are evidence of Vermont's deforestation. VHS

who was superintendant of the project. Despite the wrangling that led finally to Silloway's dismissal, a three-story building approved by Marsh arose on the old site. It was steamheated, gas-lighted and as fireproof as possible. It cost less than $150,000 and was ready for occupancy in October 1859. Architects considered it "the finest specimen of Greek architecture." It is still in use as Vermont's capitol, a handsome, golden-domed monument to Marsh's taste.

It was as Fish Commissioner that Marsh gave intimations of his later philosophy of natural history and indictment of man's treatment of land its creatures — "a little bombshell," Wallace Stegner calls it. Fishing in Vermont was now even worse than it had been in his boyhood. The Legislature had passed act after act to protect what was left, but the plump salmon, the silvery trout had all but vanished from the waters. What was wrong?

Marsh told them. Not only greedy over-fishing and dam building were the reasons, but ". . . other and more obscure causes have had a very important influence in producing the same result . . . much must doubtless be ascribed to the general physical changes produced by the clearing and cultivating of the soil. . . . It is certain that while the spring and autumnal freshets are more violent, the volume of water in the dry season is less in all our water courses than it formerly was, and there is no doubt that the summer temperature of the brooks has been elevated. . . . The clearing of the woods has been attended with the removal of many obstructions to the flow of water. . . . The general character of our water courses has become in fact more torrential. . . . In inundations, not only does the mechanical violence of the current destroy or sweep down fish and their eggs, and fill the water with mud and other impurities, but it continually changes the beds and banks of the streams, and thus renders it difficult and often impossible for the fish . . . to return to their breeding places to deposit their spawn." He goes on to say that changes in the surface of the soil involve great changes also in the food supply and kinds available to fish. "Without citing further examples, which might be indefinitely multiplied, it is enough to say that human improvements have produced an almost total change in all the external conditions of piscatorial life . . . and we must of course expect that the number of our fish will be greatly affected by these revolutions."

His report showed in all their complexity the interrelations between species and the part man played in changing the environment. It was not until 1871 that it bore fruit when, following a report of Spencer Baird, Commissioner of Fisheries, Congress appropriated money for stocking rivers and streams with "useful fish."

This was Columbia University in the 1850s, on Park Place, New York City. NYHS

The strain of earning a livelihood had been a little relieved by his commission salaries, and Marsh felt free to accept a job lecturing on the English language at Columbia University in New York, a job he felt he could take since it was only for one winter.

The course "could hardly fail to yield the professor a considerable amount in fees," wrote the university. This time, in a setting he enjoyed, among interested listeners, his talks were lively and full of fascinating sidelights, ranging from the impact of Gutenberg's press to the importance of regional dialects. But again the pay was far less than Marsh had hoped, although the small class had gone well. He would not stay another year. "The course does not pay; a business which yields no profit ought to be given up." But the winter did yield one good thing, a collection of his Columbia lectures, which received excellent reviews: it was indeed the first serious historical and morphological study of the English language. At the same time Caroline published a book of poems, *Wolfe of the Knoll,* which equaled, claimed the reviewer, "anything of Southey or Poe." In a word, winter in New York had been beneficial to them both; Caroline was now able to walk almost a quarter of a mile without pain.

The next winter, 1860, Marsh agreed to give the Lowell Lectures in Boston on the origin and history of English. After one lecture his eyes failed again and he was forced to retreat to Burlington, where he worked his notes into a book. It was a miserable winter in the little lakeside city and he felt too ill to do much more than to work in his study. He had been looking forward so much to the intellectual delights of Boston! His book, when it came out two years later as *The Origin and History of the English Language and of the Early Literature it Embodies,* was much more thorough and much less readable than the Columbia Lectures, which had gone through four printings. Altogether the Marshes' literary earnings had netted them less than $400 in three years.

Ill health pursued the family. Caroline was never quite well and young George fell ill of typhoid again. The boy had been with them in Turkey and was now at the Harvard Law School. The father rushed to his side and George pulled through, but never fully recovered. It may be that the fever affected his mind, for to his parents' consternation for the rest of his life he harbored the delusion that his father and stepmother were persecuting him. "I am sixty years old with a perfect debacle about me," wrote Marsh.

All the same, already floating about in his mind was the germ of the idea for *Man and Nature.* "I'll tell you of the book," he wrote to Baird, "well, it's a little volume showing that whereas others think the earth made man, man in fact made the earth. Now don't roll up the whites of your eyes and quote me that foolish old saw about the cobbler and his last. I am not going into the scientific, but the historicals, in which I am as good as any of you. What I put in of scientific speculations I shall steal, pretty much, but I do know some things myself. For instance, my father had a piece of thick woodland where the ground was always damp. Wild turnips grew there and ginseng and wild pepper sometimes. Well Sir, he cleaned up that lot and drained and cultivated it, and it became a good deal drier, and he raised good corn and grain on it. Now I am going to state this as a 'fact' and I defy all you speculators about cause and effect to deny it."

Too ill and harassed to go to Washington himself to seek employment from the new Lincoln Administration, he listened to friends assuring him that if he wanted a post abroad, they would back him. It was rumored, too, that certain railroad interests hoped to have him safely out of the country before he could be commissioned to write another scathing report. He did want a post, that of Minister to the newly-formed kingdom of Italy, whose capital was in Turin. He thought he could live there and support Caroline comfortably. But he feared the appointment would never be his. In despair he read that Carl Schurz, the German revolutionary and Lincoln supporter, would be the President's choice. Still, he hoped that the Italian government would not be happy with the "Dutchman," and that Lincoln would recognize that from ". . . much study of the language, history and especially the present political relation of Italy I could be more useful there than anywhere." In the end Schurz went off to Spain and Marsh, to his great delight, got the post he coveted.

It was just in time. Seven years full of despair, the years in which selfish men, as he saw it, had conspired against him, had taken their toll. "No one thought that Mr. Marsh would get it," Caroline wrote, "nothing but the feeling that Mr. Marsh was breaking down under his book-making induced us to try for this appointment. We were earning the barest living with the hardest work. Mr. Marsh's eyes were failing, and two years had made his shoulders stoop and changed him almost to an old man." His friends told Caroline they feared that under such a strain he had not much time to live.

Though he worried about leaving his son, about his unfinished books and about his country on the verge of war, Marsh flew about like a boy getting ready. Secretary Seward wanted him in Turin as soon as possible. He looked forward to living in Italy, whose people were, "inherently and collectively a civilized people." They were "noble people who have groaned for a thousand years under the direst of curses — the tyranny of the soldier and the tyranny of the priest." Marsh was to revise somewhat both his enthusiasm and his hates as he got to know the country better, but to the end of his life he regarded the Italians with affection and their country with love.

Eleven days after the outbreak of the Civil War, on April 27, 1861, Marsh sailed from his native country, never to return.

The Methodist Church, State Street, circa 1860, Burlington. UVM

THE new kingdom of Italy, to which Marsh was the first American Minister, was not yet a united state. The Austrians, "those hell-born tyrants," as Marsh called them, had been expelled from all the Italian provinces except Venice and Rome. The rest of Italy was united under the Duke of Savoy and Sardinia. Turin was the ancient ducal seat, and it was their capital which became that of the new kingdom. An austere granite city peopled by a tradition-bound society, its appeal was the spectacular view of the Alps shimmering in the distance, and ". . . Mt. Rosa, blindingly gorgeous with sunlight and snow from base to crest."

Marsh found many old diplomatic friends on hand, but Caroline was bored by the endless ritual of dinners and visits, by the stiff protocol and ancient social prejudices. The Marshes learned that only recently had it been made possible for untitled persons to occupy a box at the Theatro Regio, but now said a nobleman sadly, "We have plenty of the bourgeoisie among us, even bankers."

Marsh and Caroline must have exerted their customary charm, for at the quarters of the American Minister on Caroline's "at home day" were soon to be found everybody, high or low, in the social hierarchy except royalty. "Prince, Duchess, Marchioness, Countess, Lord, Baron — not a link missed!", Caroline wrote home. The strain of entertaining was sometimes made worse by the presence of feuding noble ladies. On one tense occasion a formidable dame, on finding her worst enemy seated in Caroline's drawing room, refused to utter a word, so that the other dozen visitors didn't say anything either. When they did speak another difficulty arose. "The deputy Salerio spent an hour with us. . . . He is full of life and intelligence — but, oh that these unhappy Turinese had something like a language! If they try to speak French, they speak bad Italian, if Italian, bad French, and one is left to divine at least half of what they would say."

King Victor Emmanuel they found charming. He was courageous and friendly, and the only complaint against him, Caroline said, was a "most unroyal passion for black bread and onions." In the brisk climate both of them prospered, Marsh looking like a man twenty years younger as his eyes became stronger. "As I am getting so strong at 63, I suppose I shall climb the Himalayas at 100," he boasted. "We are just under the Alps, and a few hours bring us to the root of them," he wrote Baird, and said that Caroline had been carried across a glacier "three hours wide" and 11,000 feet above sea level, he and a little niece trudging along side. Caroline was so much better that she was able to entertain two or three times a week, and even go to the theater. There were other social occasions. Marsh, who hadn't hunted since he was a boy in Woodstock, was once summoned by the King to join a shooting party. "There's a hare,

The Royal Palace, Turin. The shadowy figures occurred when people moved during lengthy camera exposures. BA

sir, shoot!" Marsh closed his eyes, squeezed the trigger, and to his gratified surprise, the hare dropped dead.

They had welcome visitors. Hiram Powers came to stay from Florence. Marsh's brother, Charles, came from faraway Woodstock. There were also less welcome visitors, the hordes of tourists who flocked to Europe after the war, demanding services from him as though he were their servant. They insisted that he look up their ancestors, act as hotel keeper, banker, travel agent to search for luggage gone astray, that he procure a lock of the king's hair, and forward their mail at his expense. Could he send, demanded a voyager, ". . . eight dozen bottles of *good* claret? I want it good enough to set before guests, and cheap enough to drink myself."

Insane or indigent Americans often had to be helped from Marsh's own slender purse. A frantic consul wrote, "Miss Anna C. Johnson, recommended to my care, is here in Marseilles, destitute and crazy. Inasmuch as you paid for her passage and gave her some money, can you tell me anything about her, and where I can get any money to keep her housed and clothed and fed?"

Otherwise, his duties were not onerous. There was not much diplomatic business between the two countries at first. But soon he was involved with the war raging at home. His diplomatic skills were put to good use in the task of convincing the Italian government not to recognize the Confederacy, a task made difficult by the dependence of the Italian mills on Southern cotton. The effort he made to purchase and send to the government thousands of Italian arms, thus keeping them from the hands of the Southern agents, was of the greatest help to the North. Most annoying was the task of dealing with hordes of would-be volunteers who wanted to fight for the Union, and who wanted Marsh to get them free passage to the United States and a commission as well.

Marsh, able to judge policies and actions only from afar, regarded Lincoln as an honest, amiable fool, incapable of waging a war. He was disgusted with the President for appointing incompetents as generals, but he thought even worse of his government's plan to offer the great Garibaldi a generalship. It would merely serve to point out to the world the North's lack of military leaders. Giuseppi Garibaldi, the popular hero of Europe and America, had with his ragged army of "red shirts" defeated the armies of the Holy Roman Empire, thrown off the hated yoke of Austria, and united the provinces of Italy. In fact, the American plan involved Marsh in a ludicrous and embarrassing misunderstanding with the fiery Italian.

In Washington, those who wanted the general on their side instructed the Minister to Belgium, Henry Sanford, to go to Italy and with the help of Marsh persuade Garibaldi to join the Northern forces as a Major-General. The two diplomats, knowing Garibaldi, thought it wise to sound out the situation first and sent Marsh's secretary to talk to the General in very broad terms. But Sanford and Marsh didn't know that one Quiggle, a consul in Belgium, had already written to Garibaldi, saying that the President wanted him to be Commander-in-Chief of all the Northern armies! Aghast, Marsh and Sanford received a message from Garibaldi that he was willing to accept the offer and was "immediately at your disposal, provided the conditions are those which your messenger had verbally indicated to me." Marsh rushed to charter a steamer to carry Sanford to the general's island home off the Sardinian coast to try to explain, but Garibaldi would have none of it. He would be Commander-in-Chief, or he wouldn't go. Privately, Marsh was relieved, and wrote to Washington that Garibaldi was so used to command and was gifted "with such an unusual temperament" that to think he would ever accept any but top position was inconceivable. To Marsh's embarrassment, the story of the confused imbroglio came out, putting him in the role of a bumbling diplomat.

Guiseppi Garibaldi, whose dramatic liberation of Italy captured the world's imagination. When the Lincoln administration proposed his joining the Union Army Garibaldi said he would be Commander-in-Chief or nothing. BA

Though the climate and the society suited George and Caroline, the old money question continued to haunt him. Living in Italy was not as inexpensive as he had hoped. His salary of $12,000 was barely sufficient, and as before in Turkey, the European diplomats cut a much better figure than did the poverty-stricken American Minister. His landlord evicted him from the cold, cramped apartment when he refused to pay $400 extra, and he had to move his family to a hotel near Genoa, four hours away by train from the capital.

In this seaside resort, on weekends, he turned again to the "little volume" he had started in Burlington, the book that was to become his most significant work, *Man and Nature or, Physical Geography as Modified by Human Action.*

For 63 years he had been inwardly digesting what he had seen as a youth in Vermont, as well as on his travels in the Near East and in Europe. Since the age of five, when he had driven with his father about the Vermont hills, the significance of watersheds and their vegetation had been clear to him. Trees retained moisture and prevented soil from washing down the slopes. Careless deforestation led to erosion, flooding and drought. He read clearly the story of man's interference in the ruined hills of Greece and Turkey. It was time now that his acute perceptions, his vast stores of information should be brought together so that men could understand what they had done to the earth.

Marsh set the scene with a short history of the lands about the Mediterranean, the area where he believed man's destructiveness was first manifested. "The Roman Empire at the period of its greatest expansion comprised the regions of the earth most distinguished by a happy combination of physical advantages." He painted in poetic vein a picture of the Garden of Eden that was the basin of the Mediterranean and its dependencies. He rhapsodized over "The luxuriant harvests of cereals that waved on every field from the shores of the Rhine to the banks of the Nile, the vines that festooned the hillsides of Syria, of Italy, and of Greece, the olives of Spain, the fruits of the Garden of the Hesperides. But . . . almost 2,000 years later, half of that paradise," he wrote, "is either deserted of civilized man and surrendered to hopeless desolation . . . vast forests have disappeared from mountain spurs and ridges . . . the vegetable earth . . . and the mould of the upland fields are washed away . . . rivers famous in history and song have shrunk to humble brooklets." The cause? "Man's ignorant disregard of the laws of nature."

In the second chapter, "The Transfer, Modification and Extirpation of Vegetable and Animal Species," he fully developed his thesis that man himself was a geological agent. He was the first to do so, and was considered by many as a radical crank. The conventional idea held by his contemporaries, the geographers Guyot and Ritter, was that the physical aspect of the earth was entirely the result of natural phenomena, mountains, rivers, oceans. "No," said Marsh, "Man is everywhere a disturbing agent. Wherever he plants his foot, the harmonies of nature are turned to discords." Even so seemingly simple an

In Vermont, as in the Holy Land, overgrazing could lead to problems. VHS

action as transporting a plant to a new soil introduces a new geographical force upon it and interferes with the growth of the native plants about it. Consider the effect of the introduction of the countless numbers of domestic animals upon the geography of the North American Continent. "The ox, the horse, the sheep and even the comparatively useless dog and cat, as well as several species of poultry, are voluntarily transported by every emigrant colony, and they soon multiply to numbers very far exceeding those of the wild genera most nearly corresponding to them . . . it is evident that the wild quadrupeds of North America, even when most numerous, were few compared with their domestic successors, and that they required a much less supply of vegetable food, and consequently were far less important as geographical elements than the many millions of hoofed and horned cattle now fed by civilized man on the same continent."

Another novel and revolutionary idea was his recognition of the involved relationships in nature. ". . . All nature is linked together by invisible bonds and every organic creature, however low, however feeble, however dependent, is necessary to the well-being of some other among the myriad forms of life with which the Creator has peopled the earth."

It was in the third chapter that Marsh examined the influence of forests on vegetation, soil and water, and his conclusions became the most influential part of the book.

"As soon as multiplying man had filled the open grounds along the margin of the rivers, the lakes, and sea, and sufficiently peopled the natural meadows and savannas of the interior, where such existed, he could find room for expansion and further growth only by the removal of a portion of the forest that hemmed him in. The destruction of the woods then was man's first conquest, his first violation of the harmonies of inanimate nature."

Marsh goes on to consider trees as conductors of heat, trees in summer and winter, the forest and its place in literature, Royal Forests and game laws, and compares American and European trees.

Every aspect of the tree is dicussed, but particularly important is the section that deals with the forest and its role in protecting the earth.

It could not be proved, he said, that trees increase rainfall, but they do maintain a more uniform degree of humidity. Their vegetable mold drinks up the rain and distributes the water more evenly. The snow cover in the woods holds and protects the soil from freezing deeply, so the melting spring snow percolates more gently downward, preventing disastrous floods. Where there are forests, tree, bird, man, beast and fish exist together in harmony.

A few ancient cedars of Lebanon are all that remain of a once densely forested area. LOC

In speaking of the consequence of the destruction of the forest, Marsh is at his most eloquent. "With the disappearance of the forest, all is changed. At one season, the earth parts with its warmth by radiation to an open sky, receives at another an immoderate heat from the unobstructed rays of the sun. Hence the climate becomes excessive, and the soil is alternately parched by the fervors of summer and seared by the rigors of winter. Bleak winds sweep unresisted over its surface, drift away the snow that sheltered it from frost and dry up its scanty moisture . . . the melting snows and vernal rains, no longer absorbed by a loose and bibulous vegetable mold, rush over the frozen surface and pour down the valleys seaward instead of filling a retentive bed of absorbent earth, and storing up a supply of moisture to feed the perennial springs. . . . The face of the earth is no longer a sponge, but a dust heap. . . . The earth, stripped of its vegetable glebe, grows less and less protective . . . and consequently less able to shield itself from wind and sun and scouring rain. . . . Gradually it becomes altogether barren and thus the earth is rendered no longer fit for the habitation of man."

"The Waters" deals with hydrological engineering projects, and in the chapter, "The Sands," he discusses the control of dunes. The last chapter, "Projected or Possible Geographical Changes by Man," gives Marsh an opportunity to speculate and warn against any vast plans to change the face of earth. ". . . in the vocabulary of nature, little and great are terms of comparison only; she knows no trifles, and her laws are as inflexible in dealing with an atom as with a continent or a planet."

Unlike Thoreau, who believed any action that altered the wilderness was evil, Marsh was not averse to man's activity. A canal across Cape Cod would end the dangerous outer passage. The Suez Canal would bring Asia and Europe closer. In such cases he believed that the beneficial results to humans outweighed any possibly adverse ecological effects. But his warning was clear; man must not act ignorantly. He must be aware of the consequences and make reasoned judgments in the most informed manner possible.

He cautioned also that government must regulate and control such actions, lest greedy men use them for selfish and harmful ends. As before in his report as Railroad Commissioner, he preferred the lesser evil of bureaucracy to the certain harms of untrammelled free enterprise. He recognized that the land, the air and the water belonged to everyone; no one must be allowed to use any of these selfishly or ruin them for others.

Man and Nature came out in 1864 and got off to a slow start. Expecting the same dismal sales record as his other books, Marsh gave the copyright as a charitable gesture to the United States Sanitary Commission, a Civil War philanthropy. Luckily, friends with a better business sense bought it back for $500 and returned it to the author. Within a few months Scribners was reprinting the book. In London it was brought out simultaneously with the New York edition. Italy had to wait until 1869 to read *Man and Nature,* but the French edition never appeared, partly due to Marsh's exacting standards. A new American and English edition was printed in 1874 and a third, posthumously, in 1885. On the centenary in 1964 of the first appearance of *Man and Nature,* Harvard University Press reprinted the text of the first edition, subsequently bringing it out in paperback format.

It was a pioneer in its field. No one had ever pointed out the total effect of all the works of man. No one had ever before turned to the study of the earth as the home of mankind. Others had voiced concern about the silted rivers, deforested hills, but only Marsh saw the *total* interdependency of the environmental and social relationships. The 18th Century naturalists had considered man's action as beneficial, order and cultivation being wrested from chaos. Marsh knew better. But the prospect was not hopeless. With man's scientific knowledge and technological advances restoration was possible. Modern conservation is based on the practical application of his theories.

The year that *Man and Nature* came out marked a change in national policy; Marsh's book doubtless crystallized opposition to the government's detrimental land proposals. Yosemite was ceded to California to be made a park, and in 1872, Yellowstone, the first National Park, was established. By the end of the century the notion of dedicating wild lands to forestry and recreation was an established idea.

The only serious omission in *Man and Nature* is the failure to deal with the exhaustion of natural resources. At that time there was no reason to think that America's resources could ever be depleted. It must be remembered that the full impact of the change from an agricultural to an industrial economy was just beginning. The use of coal in large amounts, the drilling of gas and oil wells, came only after the end of the Civil War. In Marsh's time, the devastation of the forests was the foremost evil. But the main theme of *Man and Nature* is not obscured by the omission of future evils; the principle remains constant: man must learn to control himself, to restore where he has destroyed, to replace where he has reaped. As Marsh grew older, he was less and less sure that this would be done.

The unification of Italy moved on. Rome was eventually to be gathered into the kingdom, but during the years 1865-1871 the Italian capital was in Florence. Marsh grumbled about the cost of moving (the State Department refusing to defray the expenses), but when they found themselves in the spacious and comfortable Villa Forini they were happier than they had even been, except for the terrible news of George's death.

Just before Lincoln was assassinated, Marsh learned that George had died in New York City. He had never fully recovered from his second bout of typhoid while at Harvard; he had done badly in his job in a law firm, had been drafted into the Army and discharged for ill health. Thereupon he started to drink heavily and ended up living in a boarding house on a small allowance that his father scraped together. His landlady wrote that the boy died railing against his father's mistreatment and cruelties.

Marsh was devastated. For weeks he could scarcely eat or sleep; his eyes failed again. Friends assured him that the boy had been of unsound mind, but Marsh agonized at the thought that he had been in some way responsible for George's death, that he had failed as a father. He had expected much from the boy and had shown him only the face of a stern disciplinarian, not that of a comforting, loving parent.

As if to make up for his treatment of George, he and Caroline indulged themselves in shamelessly spoiling an adopted Swedish boy, whom they had rescued from a crazed American foster mother living in Rome. "Prince Karl" they called him. "I do not know whether Mrs. Marsh mentioned to you a little Swedish trovatello, whom singular circumstances have thrown into our hands. He is the second child whom we have been instrumental in rescuing from the cruel treatment by an insane American woman. He is now two and a half years old, and is very intelligent and attractive. . . ."

Karl or "Carlo," as he called himself, came back to America with Caroline after Marsh's death but alas, the attractive intelligent lad turned into a scrapegrace youth and eventually disappeared from sight.

As always, Marsh's relations with young people were warm and sensitive. His youthful aides served him with devotion and loyalty, while flocks of nieces and nephews vied with each other to be chosen to live in Italy with Aunt Caroline and Uncle George.

The years in Florence brought them both better health. Their good friend, Dr. Elizabeth Blackwell, advised Caroline to see Dr. J. Marion Sims in Paris. She did so; a benign uterine tumor was removed and Marsh said ". . . if she would hold still for a couple of months, she would be as good as cured." As for him, a new oculist and a new pair of glasses restored his failing vision.

Young Swedish Karl poses with his adoptive father who happily spoiled the boy. WHS

His library was shipped from Vermont and housed in the rambling villa. Caroline gave weekly teas and dinners, and their bedrooms were constantly filled with visitors from America and new friends from Britain. Matthew Arnold, the Brownings, Trollope and George Eliot called on them, to sit on the broad loggias overlooking the Arno.

Marsh's greatest concern now was that he might be ousted from his post. The usual scramble for office followed Lincoln's reelection. Marsh wrote, "I hear the cheep of the axe which shall lop my official head from my shoulders, and I shall not regret my removal were it not that I have no other source of income left and were I to return to America I should not know how to get a living." There was nothing at home to call him back. His family was dispersed, his brothers dead, his boyhood home in Woodstock had been purchased by the railroad magnate, Frederick Billings and transformed into a Queen Anne villa. His books were all in Florence; it would cost a fortune to ship them back again. Vermont winters suited neither of them. "In this climate," Marsh said, "my

chances of life double what they would be at home. For an old man, a solitary life is more enjoyable and fruitful here than in America."

When Lincoln was assassinated, there was a question whether he would be continued, but Johnson, whom Marsh had known in Congress, kept him on as did Grant, who on his accession to the Presidency, removed all ministers but Marsh. The old Vermonter, firmly en-

Opposite: Marsh in his library in the Villa Forini, Florence. UVM
Above: The Ponte Vecchio, Florence, as Marsh would have seen it. NYPL
Below: Looking up the Arno through the arches of the famous bridge. PL

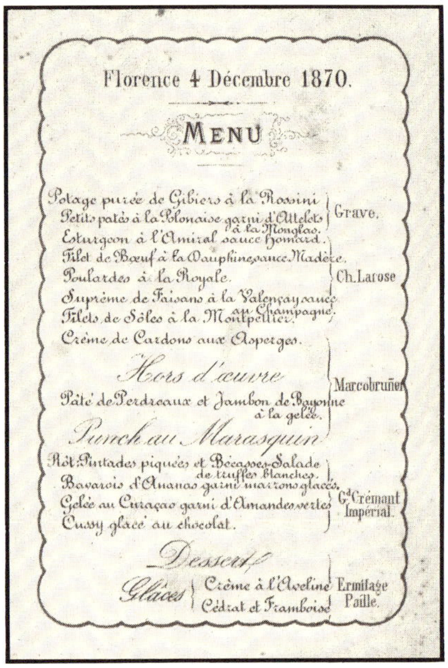

Florence 4 Décembre 1870.

MENU

Potage purée de Gibiers à la Rossini
Petits patés à la Polonaise garni d'Attelets à la Monglas.
Esturgeon à l'Amiral sauce homard.
Filet de Bœuf à la Dauphine, sauce Madère.
Poulardes à la Royale.
Suprême de Faisans à la Valençay sauce au Champagne.
Filets de Sôles à la Montpellier.
Crème de Cardons aux Asperges.

Grave.
Ch. Larose

Hors d'œuvre

Pâté de Perdreaux et Jambon de Bayonne à la gelée.

Marcobruñer

Punch au Marasquin

Rôt: Pintades piquées et Bécasses-Salade de truffes blanches.
Bavarois d'Ananas garni marrons glacés.
Gelée au Curaçao garni d'Amandes vertes
Cussy glacé au chocolat.

Gd Crémant Impérial.

Dessert

Glâces | Crème à l'Aveline
Cédrat et Framboise

Ermitage Paille.

Top: Robert Browning, BA *and his wife, Elizabeth Barrett Browning,* LOC, *sketched by the British artist Field Talfourd in Rome, 1859. Center: menu for a dinner given by King Victor Emmanuel, Florence, 4 December 1870* DL *Bottom:* Cartes de Visitez, *Niece Carrie Crane, Brother Charles Marsh and, standing, Hiram Powers. All* DL

Rome in the 1870's; the church of Trinita de Monti, above the Flower Market on the Spanish Steps, Rome. BA

trenched, completed twenty-one years as a diplomat, the longest tour of duty in the history of the American Foreign Service. He was able to meet the tiring demands of the office with the help of his invaluable secretary, G. W. Wurtz, for the crowd of younger, ambitious men, hungry for office, watched him closely for signs of ineptitude, in hopes of a salutary removal. The last move came in 1871 in Rome. Marsh was 70, and it upset him, but this time his moving expenses were paid. In fact, his salary was raised, but to the end of his life the spectre of insolvency continued to haunt him. The articles he wrote for Johnson's *Universal Encyclopedia* on a vast number of subjects, ranging from the Papal Index to the manufacture of straw, were a task he delighted in, but one that was also much needed, even at $20 a page. Caroline, as always, did her part. "Mrs. Marsh has also contributed a great deal of translation and other writing," he reminded Johnson, when asking for payment. "We really need the money to meet our expenses." Caroline's work rated only $10, as against her husband's $20. In spite of these efforts,

The Rome Marsh saw and knew. Above: Pope Pius IX blesses the crowd on Easter Sunday. Below: the Piazza del Popolo.

Above: Piazza Navonne, noon on a market day. Below: The well-preserved Arch of Titus in the Forum. All pictures LLA

Marsh's indispensable secretary, George Washington Wurtz. LOC

had it not been for his brother Charles' legacy of $7300, the Marshes would have remained in debt. At one point, deeply depressed by this perpetual penury, Marsh offered his beloved library for sale at $10,000, but the price was considered too high. After his death, Frederick Billings of Woodstock bought it for $15,000 to give to his alma mater, the University of Vermont. He commissioned the famous architect, H. H. Richardson, to house it. In Woodstock, Billings, a convert to Marsh's ideas, had reforested the treeless top of Mt. Tom, the spot that had first engaged Marsh's thoughts.

Wurtz, the priceless secretary, was able to take on many of the regular duties of the Minister, yet Marsh always begrudged the time he himself must give to his official task. For him there was still so much to study and learn. He revised *Man and Nature* three times, adding further instances of man-made disturbances of the natural process. An important work of these later years was the paper written at the request of the United States Commissioner of Agriculture on irrigation. With the North American Continent crossed and the coasts linked by rail, men were greedily hoping to wrest dry land from the desert by means of irrigation. Marsh's years of study of the arid lands of the Mediterranean and ancient irrigation convinced him that while there may be benefits, there were also built-in troubles: salinity, exhausted soils, loss of nutrients. And as in his report to the Railroad Commission, and in *Man and Nature,* he warned that selfish interests would try to control water rights, that the government must be on hand to regulate the water for the benefit of all. "Acquisition of the control of abundant sources of water by private individuals may often result in the establishment of vested rights and monopolies liable to great abuse." In addition he urged that a thorough survey of the West be made to determine just what should be done to irrigate the dry territories. Just as his Fish Commission report had led to the rehabilitation of lakes and streams in Vermont and as *Man and Nature* stimulated the preservation of wilderness lands, Marsh's irrigation report was instrumental in the creation of the Bureau of Land Reclamation in 1902.

He never returned to the United States. He loved Italy, its climate, food and scenery. He had, "such a passion for the nature of Italy that I do not see how I can ever live under another sky." Although Marsh as usual fretted over expenses, an account by Mrs. Underwood of Burlington, Vermont, who dined with the Marshes in Rome, gave evidence that the American Minister did indeed live in some splendor. "They live in great style with men in full English servants' dress, who speak both English and Italian. . . . Mrs. Marsh is so very young . . . she is the most brilliant talker I have ever heard. She does not only talk well herself, but draws other people out. . . . I have always heard of Mr. Marsh as a cold man, but I have seldom been addressed with words containing sympathy and cordial sentiments like those with which he spoke."

The legation in which Mrs. Underwood was entertained was the Rospigliosi Palace, a floor of which was rented for the Marshes. "The furniture . . . though not new, is splendid, and the proportions of the

Remnants of a Roman aqueduct march across the barren Campagna. PL

Above: in Rome the Marshes occupied an entire floor of the Palazzo Rospigliosi. AA
Left: after an operation Caroline was able to fully enjoy Rome's social life. UVM
Right: From their Palazzo the Marshes looked out on the Colosseum. BA

numerous rooms are magnificent, but the great charm of it to us is the view from its windows of Rome. . . . The view of the Colosseum is unique. The unbroken side being turned towards us, it presents to us much the same appearance it did to those who saw it from the same hill (the Quirinal) eighteen centuries ago," reported Marsh, pleased with his Roman abode.

With the restoration of Caroline's health and Marsh's eyesight being restored as well, they found themselves involved in the social whirl. "Mrs. Marsh has been well enough to give two receptions a week, and I know not how many dinners." The lack of males was the perennial problem. Marsh wrote, "I hope we shall soon see your friend Mr. C . . . you describe him as being just what we are in great need of — a good diner-out. In the American society at Rome, the female persuasion is awfully redundant. Ladies come in trios and quartettes, with no male attendant. What can one do with such at a dinner table? At Mrs. Marsh's last reception appeared a *he*, accompanied by eight *she's*. How despairing!"

In the summer, when he could leave the post to Wurtz, he would escape with his family of grand-nieces and nephews to the mountains. His favorites were the Alps, the country of his dreams. "Giving up the

Leaving the summer heat of Rome the Marshes holidayed at the Italian lakes, LOC, *in the Alps,* LOC, *and in their beloved Italian countryside.* AC

Alps seems to me like giving up all the material world." In his late 70's he was still scrambling about to measure stream flow, or to assess glacial advance. While the Alps were his love, especially the Dolomites and the Swiss mountains, he felt a great affection for the Tuscan Appenines, that dramatic, rocky spine of Italy. Caroline, partner in these happy summer jaunts, put up, uncomplaining as always, with the discomforts all travelers must endure. In 1881 she relates how she and Marsh managed to sleep, both on a small cot, in a worse-than-usually equipped mountain inn. "We slept well, but first we secured the narrow short sheet and blanket intended to cover us by spreading them over and tucking them firmly in at foot and side." With Marsh's 200-pound bulk, it must have been a tight fit.

Near the very end of his life a friendship carried on by letter with young Charles Sargent, Director of the Arnold Arboretum of Harvard University, renewed his interest in forestry. Botanical observations were traded back and forth across the Atlantic which inspired Marsh, in his 79th year, to set forth once more and measure tree trunks and scrutinize leaf formations. From the Tyrol he wrote Sargent that as he was "on the retired list, he had not attempted to climb any peaks, but he had . . . crept about among the evergreens and made such observations on their growth as I was able."

In the summer of 1882, the Marshes left for Vallombrosa in the Appenines, where his friend, Alfredo di Berenger, had established a school of forestry. From the hotel nearby, Marsh should take short walks under the cool mountain pines, measuring trees, talking to the forestry students, watching the clouds form over the hot valley below.

On July 23 he arose early, began work on some additional notes to the latest edition of *Man and Nature,* then joined the family outside under the trees. That day the clouds piled in shining masses, had assumed billowing, fantastic shapes. Marsh amused the young circle about him by telling them how the clouds had been given their names and finding imaginary animals in the drifting vapor.

A little before six he suddenly felt tired, and went in to rest. When Caroline came in to see how he was, he was quietly dying. The doctor, hurriedly summoned, proclaimed as he laid down Marsh's hand, *"Ecco la morte del giusto."* "It is the death of a just man." Two days later his body, covered with flowers, was carried down the mountainside by the foresters, and buried in the Protestant Cemetery in Rome.

It was a fitting end for the man who had loved Italy, the mountains and the natural beauty around him. The avid scholar had, to the day of his death, continued to learn and to write. "He would have desired nothing different," wrote Caroline.

The village of Vallombrosa, in the Appenines, east of Florence, where Marsh died in 1882. AA

Marsh in old age. WHS

He was fortunate in having lived at a time when it was still possible to be a generalist. A student of specialized attainments could never have conceived and formed into a whole, all by himself, a concept of human geography. Only a man such as George Marsh, with his voracious mind and tremendous capacity for experience, could have dreamed of writing of the Earth as a home for man.

Marsh never thought of himself as anything but a dabbler in the realms of knowledge or as attaining a modicum of competency in anything but linguistics. He was, it is true, trained professionally in the law. But his unquenchable passion for knowing, his energy, his vast memory, and his perceptive genius enabled him to fuse together what he had seen and what he studied into *Man and Nature.*

The historian Lewis Mumford says of Marsh that his work "is the fountainhead of the conservation movement." For Stewart Udall, former Secretary of the Interior, Marsh's significance is as the "framer of the new land ethic. . . . Man was part of the cycle of nature, and the fall of a sparrow or the felling of a tree should be studied in the context of the total environment. These concepts were Marsh's most valuable contributions, and in time they became part of a saving American creed . . . with the perspective of a full century, we can perceive that his words were the beginning of land wisdom in this country."

Marsh's final resting place, in the Protestant Cemetery in Rome, UVM

This plaque was affixed to a wall of the former Woodstock home of George Perkins Marsh in 1967.

THE WORLD OF GEORGE PERKINS MARSH
was designed by Frank Lieberman, Woodstock, Vermont.
3500 Copies of the book have been set and printed
by the Whitman Press, Inc., Lebanon, N.H.
on Monadnock Caress, smooth finish paper.
The text type is 11 point Trump Medieval.
Binding by the New Hampshire Bindery, Concord, N.H.